What a strange
gruities exist in the affections and perceptions of the regenerate soul. This
introduction to the piety of the Senior and Junior Basil Manly is a fasci-
nating, moving, and shocking look at piety among Southern Baptists in the
middle two-thirds of the nineteenth century. Biographical introductions
and primary sources show the reader the beauty of the life harnessed to
the glory of God and the bewildering sense of honor displayed in the beat-
ing of a slave, an abiding sense of the eternality and transcendent claims
of the kingdom combined with a relentless southern jingoism. A carefully
stated doctrinal orthodoxy co-exists and gives rise in the same hearts to the
creative linguistic power of singable poetry. The reader of this volume will
certainly be educated, challenged, fascinated, perplexed, and led to examine
himself and take heed lest he also be tempted.
— Tom J. Nettles, Professor of Historical Theology,
The Southern Baptist Theological Seminary

The publication of these writings is long overdue and is most welcome, and
the editors have done their work well. The selections are filled with insight,
encouragement, and challenge. May readers catch the Manlys' zeal for
spreading the knowledge of the Savior, and their compassion for lost souls.
— Gregory A. Wills, Professor of Church History,
The Southern Baptist Theological Seminary

The Manly family provided Southern Baptists with two generations of lead-
ership during the nineteenth century. Basil Manly, Sr. and Basil Manly, Jr.
were pastor-theologians and pioneers in theological education among the
Baptists in the American South. This collection of their correspondence and
shorter writings evidences the evangelical Calvinistic piety that buttressed
their many accomplishments. Michael Haykin, James Fuller, and Roger
Duke have done us a service by introducing the Manlys to a new genera-
tion. Hopefully contemporary Southern Baptists and other evangelicals will
drink deeply from the same well that nourished this great family's gospel
efforts of a previous century.
— Nathan Finn, Assistant Professor of Church History,
Southeastern Baptist Theological Seminary

Few families, if any, have ever had the influence and impact on the Southern Baptist Convention as the Manly family. The introductory and biographical essays on the lives of Basil Manly, Sr., and Basil Manly, Jr., as well as the carefully selected collections from their writings found in this volume are wonderful and much-welcomed additions to Baptist studies. This collection, however, is more than a look back for church historians. These writings found in this volume continue to speak in a fresh and powerful way to the issues and trends in our contemporary churches and culture. I am quite pleased to recommend Soldiers of Christ.

— DAVID S. DOCKERY, PRESIDENT, UNION UNIVERSITY

The Church is ever in need of being reminded how sinners redeemed by the grace of God have been used to extend the kingdom of God. This selection of writings by Basil Manly, Sr. and Basil Manly, Jr. provides the historical framework for understanding their faults in light of their times and for gauging their influence to the present day. Pastors will especially be helped by this work as they look over the shoulders of two men whose ministries were met with multiple responsibilities and who themselves were marked by godly character.

— TONY CHUTE, ASSOCIATE PROFESSOR OF CHURCH HISTORY, CALIFORNIA BAPTIST UNIVERSITY

A superb collection of well-edited primary sources by two of the most formative shapers of Southern Baptist life in the nineteenth century. The brilliance, vision, passion, and faults of Basil Manly, father and son, come through with clarity in these historic documents, shedding much needed light on Southern culture and Baptist history.

—TIMOTHY GEORGE, FOUNDING DEAN OF BEESON DIVINITY SCHOOL OF SAMFORD UNIVERSITY AND A SENIOR EDITOR OF CHRISTIANITY TODAY

Basil Manly

&

Basil Manly, Jr.

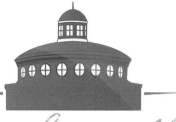

Truth. Legacy. Vision.

SOUTHERN SEMINARY
SESQUICENTENNIAL

150 YEARS

"Soldiers of Christ"
SELECTIONS FROM THE WRITINGS OF BASIL MANLY, SR., & BASIL MANLY, JR.

Michael A. G. Haykin,
Roger D. Duke,
and A. James Fuller

Foreword by
R. Albert Mohler, Jr.

Founders Press
Committed to historic Baptist principles
Cape Coral, Florida

Published by

Founders Press

Committed to historic Baptist principles
P.O. Box 150931 • Cape Coral, FL 33915
Phone (239) 772-1400 • Fax: (239) 772-1140
Electronic Mail: founders@founders.org
Website: http://www.founders.org

ISBN 978-0-9785711-7-7

To

Dr. R. Albert Mohler, Jr.,

With thanks to God for his faithfulness
to the vision and piety of the founders
of the Southern Baptist Theological Seminary

Contents

Selections from Basil Manly, Sr.

Selections from Basil Manly, Jr.

Foreword

Humanly speaking, the formula is easy: no Manlys, no Southern Seminary. This year, as the Southern Baptist Theological Seminary celebrates its sesquicentennial, our indebtedness to the Manlys of South Carolina is increasingly clear. As an institution, our history is inextricably tied to the lives and ministries of Basil Manly, Sr. and Basil Manly, Jr.

Every institution has a biography, and the biography of Southern Seminary reaches back to Charleston, South Carolina. The ministry of Basil Manly, Sr. as pastor of the First Baptist Church of Charleston roots that family in the most historic church among the Baptists of the South. But the First Baptist Church of Charleston was not merely influential because of its historic role as the first Baptist congregation of the South. The Charleston church was itself the source of a theological river that runs through the center of Southern Baptist life and gave birth to the Southern Baptist Theological Seminary. The "Charleston Tradition" is more than a matter of historical interpretation. The faith, the confession, and the theological conviction that gave birth to Southern Seminary was one nurtured and embraced by Basil Manly, Sr. as he served as pastor to the congregation and thus as pastor to the family that would produce James Petigru Boyce.

Taken together, Basil Manly, Sr. and Basil Manly, Jr. represent something like the grandfather and father to Southern Seminary. As the first chairman (then president) of Southern Seminary's Board of Trustees, Basil Manly, Sr. wielded an enormous personal influence. His determination that Southern Seminary be an institution that was accountable to the local church and regulated by a confession is central to Southern Seminary's story. Without the stature of a leader like Basil Manly, Sr., the idea of a central seminary for Baptists in the South might have remained just that—an idea.

Basil Manly, Jr., following in the tradition and heritage of his father, was essential to the composition of Southern Seminary's first faculty. This becomes clear when it is understood that he, along with James Petigru Boyce, represented half of Southern Seminary's first faculty. Thus, the First Baptist Church of Charleston and the ministry of Basil Manly, Sr. provided fully half of the quartet that established the school. Basil Manly, Jr. was instrumental in the composition of Southern Seminary's confession of faith, the Abstract of Principles. He was no mere editor. To the contrary, the Abstract of Principles represents a theological achievement for which Basil Manly, Jr. deserves first credit. When the seminary confronted its first theological crisis, it was Professor Manly who responded with *The Bible Doctrine of Inspiration*, clearly articulating this institution's uncompromising stance on behalf of plenary inspiration, inerrancy, and infallibility of the Bible. But, like his father, Basil Manly, Jr. was a man of many talents and gifts. As a hymnist, he wrote some of the most important hymns of the Baptist tradition, including Southern Seminary's own hymn, "Soldiers of Christ in Truth Arrayed." Thus, Basil Manly, Jr. provided the only words written by one of our founders that continue to resound in the voices of Southern Seminary's students and faculty at every convocation and graduation.

Both of the Manlys were creatures of their time. One of the achievements of *Soldiers of Christ* is to present the lives and writings of the Manlys in a way that is intellectually honest and academically responsible. As those behind this project indicate, we learn from their piety and convictions, even as we stand in a very different place and live in a very different time.

You will find rich sustenance in this book. In the writings of Basil Manly, Sr. and Basil Manly, Jr. we find two of the greatest minds ever to serve the Southern Baptist Convention and to contribute to American and religious life. Their deep piety, unquestioned conviction, and faithful churchmanship set them apart, even in their own day. Now, a new generation is afforded the opportunity of learning more faithfully how to praise and honor God as we are instructed together by this faithful father and son.

— R. Albert Mohler, Jr.

Louisville, Kentucky

Preface

The history of Christian piety is ever the history of sinners redeemed by grace, seeking to live lives that honor God—and falling short. They are saints, to be sure, inextricably a part of God's kingdom that is breaking into the realm of history, their lives prefiguring the full disclosure at the end of time of that city whose designer and builder is God. But they are not there yet, and the best of these saints experiences the marring of sin as an ongoing reality in this age. The support of Basil Manly, Sr., for the institution of slavery well reveals this perennial struggle with sin.

Now, one of Manly's earliest pronouncements about slavery, "On the Emancipation of Slaves,"[1] can be interpreted as an antislavery document.[2] During most of his career, however, he was pro-slavery, though he ever detested the abuses of the South's "peculiar institution."[3] There is clear evidence that after the Civil War, though, his attitude towards African-Americans changed signifi-

---

1. For a selection from this work, see below, pages 61–67.
2. See below, though, for the debate on this, page 61 n. 1.
3. See Janet Duitsman Cornelius, *Slave Missions and The Black Church in the Antebellum South* (Columbia: University of South Carolina Press, 1999), 42–43, and also below, pages 83–84, 105–107.

cantly.[4] On December 1, 1868, only three weeks before his death and the very last time that he spoke to the students of the Southern Baptist Theological Seminary, where his son and namesake was then teaching and which the elder Manly had played a role in founding,[5] he shared his testimony of conversion. In it he recorded the way that a pious slave was the means of his conversion and he left the Southern students with a picture of him as a young man humbly kneeling side by side with this African-American brother.[6]

Despite the difficulties posed by this element of the elder Manly's life — it is balanced by the younger Manly's more biblical perspective in "Our Brother in Black" — this book has been such a blessing to compose. In this sesqui-centennial year of the founding of the Southern Baptist Theological Seminary, it is with a deep sense of gratitude to God that the professors and students at the Southern Baptist Theological Seminary should look back to the theological clarity and rich piety of the founders — James Petigru Boyce; Basil Manly, Jr.; John A. Broadus; and William Williams. And we need to be thankful to God that

---

4. Cornelius, *Slave Missions and The Black Church*, 207–208. Cornelius finds partial evidence for this in the document "Our Brother in Black," which she attributes to the elder Manly. This attribution is probably mistaken (see below, page 203 n. 1), though her statement about the change in Manly is not.

5. See below, pages 98–104.

6. A. James Fuller, *Chaplain to the Confederacy: Basil Manly and Baptist Life in the Old South* (Baton Rouge: Louisiana State University Press, 2000), 11–12, and below, pages 3–4.

He has used Dr. R. Albert Mohler, Jr., to whom this small book has been dedicated, to lead the school back to a position that harmonizes with all that is biblical in the piety of these founders!

— Michael A. G. Haykin

Louisville, Kentucky
March 9, 2009

Acknowledgments

In writing this book, A. James Fuller was responsible for the introductory essay on Basil Manly, Sr., and all of the selections from his writings. He would like to thank Michael O'Brien for an introduction to Basil Manly many years ago and Brenda Fuller for her love and patience with an all-consuming project in the midst of trial.

Roger D. Duke edited many of the selections from the younger Manly's writings, while Michael A. G. Haykin drew up the introductory essay on Basil Manly, Jr., and did the overall editing of the book. For help in preparing that introductory essay and the selections from the younger Manly's writings, Haykin and Duke would like to express their indebtedness to Dr. Gregory A. Wills and Rev. Carl L. Stam of the Southern Baptist Theological Seminary; Mr. Jason Fowler, the archivist of the Southern Baptist Theological Seminary, and his assistant, Mr. Chris Dewease; Dr. David Gregory, music and A.V. librarian at the Southern Baptist Theological Seminary and three of his assistants, Charles Priest, Andrew Wymer, and Chris Fenner; Kevin Davis, the library exhibits coordinator at the James P. Boyce Centennial Library at the Southern Baptist Theological Seminary; Dr. Jeff Robinson;

Dr. Peter Beck of Charleston Southern University, Charleston, South Carolina; and Rev. Steve Weaver, Michael Haykin's research assistant at the Andrew Fuller Center for Baptist Studies. We would also like to thank Bill Sumners, director of the Southern Baptist Historical Library and Archives, Nashville, Tennessee, for his research assistance.

Louisville, Kentucky
March 9, 2009

When once the path of duty, to God or his fellowmen, appears, [the Christian] will raise no questions of preference, of ease, or accommodations; he has no will but to do the will of his Father which is in Heaven, and to finish his work.... Love, unconquerable love, seizes and occupies the breast, irradiates, ennobles, and strengthens the mind, and implants in the bosom an impulse to do good, which shakes off all impediments, overcomes the defects of education and the embarrassments of condition, seizes and employs every facility, presses into the service all the aids of learning, station, character, and all the little wealth it can command, together with every kind and degree of natural and spiritual attainment, and offers all as a tribute to the glory of Christ in the regeneration of mankind.

— Basil Manly, Sr. (1841)

No one could preach the Gospel more freely than [Basil Manly, Sr.]. No one ever urged sinners more earnestly and successfully to believe in Christ as their Saviour. No one felt more than he the duty to give to every man a message, as sent from God to him.... He was what the Bible describes as a Christian, full of humility and charity.

— J. P. Boyce (funeral sermon
for Basil Manly, Sr., 1868)

We are nearing home. Every day brings us nearer to laying down the burden, & taking up the crown, if indeed we have been made meet by divine grace to be "partakers of the inheritance of the saints in light.*" What a world that will be! A world of* saints *— no sin there; none of the imperfections which taint & mar the best here; of saints in light — here even the holy walk often in darkness, much in woe & tribulations, sometimes in doubts & fears — but there it will be in unfading, & inexpressible light, the glorious light of God.*

— Basil Manly, Jr. (1869)

[Basil Manly, Jr.] made an impression upon students, as he did upon people who knew him in other relations, of extraordinary saintliness of character, purity of life, and of gentle strength.

— W. O. Carver

Basil Manly, Sr.

A song of mercy and judgment:
The piety of Basil Manly, Sr.
(1798–1868)

by A. James Fuller

Lying on his deathbed, the dying preacher considered the course of his life in light of God's mercy and judgment. Basil Manly believed that these two disparate strands of divine providence could be synthesized in the doctrine of Christian duty, and he had worked to fulfill the responsibility of his calling as an individual, a husband and father, a master and planter, a minister and educator. Further, the Southern Baptist struggled with the tension between the ethic of honor that served as an underpinning of his society and the piety demanded by his Christian faith. Again, duty was his reconciliation, as he brought together faith and honor in a concept of Christian gentility. In 1832, he had delivered a sermon on the history of the First Baptist Church of Charleston, South Carolina, based on Psalm 101:1, "I will sing of mercy and judgment, unto thee, O Lord, will I sing." Entitled *Mercy and Judgment*, the sermon contained his belief that "mercy and judgment, either mingled or alternate, make up the history of our lives — fill the records of churches and of States." Looking back now, he saw both mercy and judgment in his own experience, since he had been pious and had fallen short of the mark; he had done his duty in ways that brought both success and failure. Now, in 1868, he reflected on his life as his family and friends gathered round him in his last hours.[1]

When a friend asked him, "How do you feel now at the prospect of life's close?" he replied, "I have been for some time in a very calm and pleasant frame of mind. I have no raptures; I have no fears; I am waiting my Master's will." He repeated his calm assurance a few hours later in talking to his son and namesake, Basil Manly, Jr. (1825–1892): "I don't want to live and I don't want to die. There is nothing for me to live for, nothing special to regret. I do not believe that God will renounce me, and give me over to dread." Asked, "How does Jesus seem to you now?" he answered, "Christ is precious to me. I have been in the habit that He will never fail to be a resource to them that trust Him." His wife asked, "And you feel that you can trust Him now?" Manly replied, "Yes…I feel willing to trust Him now, with my soul and all, to live or to die as seems good to Him." Not long after, as noon approached on December 21, 1868, he brought his reflections to an end: "I have not found, nor do I consider it true, that life was a failure. Taking up Jesus as the aim of life, there is sufficient to support a man, and life is a reality indeed, and not a failure. I would be willing, with Him, to live life over. But I am willing to go or stay, as

---

1. For a full biography, see A. James Fuller, *Chaplain to the Confederacy: Basil Manly and Baptist Life in the Old South* (Baton Rouge: Louisiana State University Press, 2000). For his delivery of *Mercy and Judgment*, see Fuller, *Chaplain to the Confederacy*, 89–105.

pleases Him." Minutes later, he uttered his last words, "O Lord, have mercy!"[2]

The piety of Basil Manly developed in the context of his life's experience. To be sure, the Baptist minister engaged the question of the Christian life in his thought and expressed his ideas in public sermons and addresses. But his piety must be judged in the course of his life and career. He filled the pulpit as pastor of several important churches, served as president of the University of Alabama, helped form the Southern Baptist Convention, spoke openly on political matters, and led his denomination's educational efforts. His private concerns also served as the framework for his Christian experience, as he worked to fulfill his duties as a husband, father, friend, and master. In the end, he died expressing an unshakable faith, assured in his reconciliation of mercy and judgment, honor and Christianity, in duty.

Early life and career

Born in 1798 in North Carolina, Basil Manly was converted in 1814. Influenced by the recent conversion of his mother, who had become a Baptist against the wishes of his Roman Catholic father, the young man began to consider his own spiritual state. Under conviction, the sixteen-year-old wandered through a cornfield, only to

---

2. Basil Manly, Jr., to brothers, December 21, 1868, Manly Family Papers, William Stanley Hoole Special Collections Library, University of Alabama, Tuscaloosa. This collection of documents is henceforth cited simply as Manly Family Papers. For more on Manly's death, see Fuller, *Chaplain to the Confederacy*, 314–315.

hear a voice in the distance. Drawing closer, he discovered an old slave man on his knees in the corn, praying for the soul of "Mas Baz." Overwhelmed with emotion, Manly knelt down beside the slave and began to pray for repentance. From that day on, Basil Manly was a Christian.[3]

Soon after, he received his calling to the ministry and hoped to pursue an education to prepare him for the Lord's work. But his father resisted this goal, telling his son that if he would "enter any honorable or profitable profession," he would pay for it, but he would have "no hand in trying to make him a Baptist preacher." If Basil pursued the ministry, his father warned that he would "scratch a poor man's back the rest of his days." Discouraged, the young man turned to his mother, who advised him well: "Do your duty, my son. I asked the Lord for your soul, when you were but a baby; and now that He has given you to me in the gospel, God forbid that I should withhold you from any service to Him." Thus encouraged, he began to study and practice preaching under the guidance of an older minister. Soon after, his father heard him preach and changed his mind, offering to pay for his education for the ministry. And so young Manly went off to study at South Carolina College in Columbia.[4]

On completing his degree at the college in 1821, he

3. Basil Manly, Jr., and Charles Manly, "Fifty Years with the Southern Baptists; or The Life and Times of Basil Manly, Sr.," Basil Manly, Jr., Papers, South Carolina Baptist Historical Collection, James Buchanan Duke Library, Furman University, Greenville, S.C.

4. Louise Manly, *The Manly Family: An Account of the Descendants of Captain Basil Manly of the Revolution and Related Families* (Greenville, S.C.: Keys Printing, 1930), 81–89.

moved to the rural Edgefield District of South Carolina to begin his ministry. Based at Little Stevens' Creek
Church, he served several congregations, working as a
circuit preacher by speaking to each in a regular rota-
tion. Infamous for violence and the independent spirit of
its inhabitants, the Edgefield District posed a challenge
for the young preacher. The planters and farmers showed
little interest in religion, and the isolation of the dispersed
population made it difficult to build a church. But Manly
soon won a reputation for his preaching ability as revival
swept through the district and eventually spilled over into
surrounding areas and into Georgia. The Baptist preacher
baptized hundreds of new converts and attracted the
attention of denominational leaders across the country.
Edgefield also brought him a wife, since he married Sarah
Rudulph and started a family.[5]

The First Baptist Church of Charleston

One man who recognized the young man's ability was
Richard Furman (1755–1825), a respected church leader
who served as pastor of the First Baptist Church of
Charleston, South Carolina.[6] Furman handpicked Manly
to be his successor and, after his death, the young minister moved to fill his place. The so-called "mother church"
of Southern Baptists, First Baptist gave Manly a platform
not only for preaching the gospel but for national leadership. In his tenure at the church, he took up Furman's

---

5. Fuller, *Chaplain to the Confederacy*, 43–55.
6. On Furman, see below, page 94 n. 9.

Richard Furman (1755–1825)

mantle by leading the denomination at the state, regional, and national levels. He worked hard to support the organizations dedicated to missions, led the movement for Baptist education in the South, and spoke on issues of both theological and political importance.[7]

Manly soon earned the respect of his fellow clergymen and a place in the intellectual life of the city. This included membership in the Literary and Philosophical Society, an organization of Charleston's men of letters. They met regularly to hear different speakers on a wide variety of subjects. Sometimes they heard outsiders but more often listened to other members give lectures. Manly spoke on a number of occasions before the society, delivering addresses on scientific subjects that also touched on social and political issues.[8]

One issue that arose while Manly worked in Charleston involved states' rights. The Nullification Crisis arose when South Carolinians led by John C. Calhoun (1782–1850), who served as Vice President of the United States under two different administrations, argued that a state had the right to nullify or veto national law. Focused on the Tariff of 1828, the battle over nullification threatened Civil War as President Andrew Jackson (1767–1845) vowed to uphold the law and South Carolina staunchly defended the right to nullify it. The governor mustered the militia while Congress passed the Force Bill authorizing the president to raise an army to enforce the law. Eventu-

7. Fuller, *Chaplain to the Confederacy*, 53.
8. Fuller, *Chaplain to the Confederacy*, 56 – 88, 106 –129.

ally, leaders like Henry Clay (1777–1852) of Kentucky and
Daniel Webster (1782–1852) of New Hampshire forged a
compromise that averted the crisis. A devoted Democrat
and supporter of Jackson, Manly sided with Calhoun and
the Nullifiers. He cast a states' rights ballot in the state
elections and, when he inadvertently left his handwritten
ballot at the polls, word of his vote spread quickly. The
state, city, and even his own congregation were divided on
the issue, and the preacher became embroiled in political
controversy. He remained a staunch supporter of states'
rights and marked the Nullification Crisis as the time
when he began to believe in a separate Southern nation.[9]

The foundation of his thinking about separatism
rested firmly on the issue of slavery. Other differences
existed and were important, but all were secondary to
the so-called "peculiar institution" of slavery. Like many
of his fellow Southerners, Manly held pro-slavery views.
But his thought on the subject developed over time and
was much more complex than might be expected. In 1821,
in the aftermath of the Missouri Compromise, he delivered a speech to the debating society at South Carolina
College entitled, "On the Emancipation of Slaves."[10] Historians continue to debate the proper interpretation of this
speech. On the surface, it seems that Manly was clearly
arguing for the emancipation and colonization of slaves.
This could certainly be the case, since the American Colonization Society continued to enjoy widespread Southern

9. Fuller, *Chaplain to the Confederacy*, 102–104.
10. For a selection from this work, see below, pages 61–67.

support at the time, and many opponents of slavery thought the plan for returning freed slaves to Africa was the only alternative to continuing the institution of slavery. Yet Manly also hinted strongly in the opening lines of the speech that he might be playing the devil's advocate, arguing one side of the issue for the sake of debate. Still another interpretation is based on the closing section of his speech, where he argued that, if colonization was not possible or practical, then slavery had to be continued. This could mean that he was actually defending slavery rather than attacking it. Whatever the case, the speech served as his first recorded statement on the volatile moral issue that would continue to demand his attention over the years.[11]

As a preacher, Manly led congregations that consisted of black majorities. Thus he faced the reality of ministering to large numbers of individuals living in bondage. One example where he came face to face with the realities of slavery was the case of Lydia Frierson. A church member who had been converted and baptized by Manly, Lydia came to him seeking help. Her master continually forced

---

11. Fuller, *Chaplain to the Confederacy*, 32–36. For a less complicated view of Manly's thought on slavery, see Harold Wilson, "Basil Manly, Apologist for Slavocracy," *Alabama Review*, 15 (January 1962): 38–53. For a study that argues that Manly actually believed in emancipation at the time of his college speech, see Shawn Ritenour, "Human Slavery and the Southern Baptist Mind" (unpublished ms. presented at the Austrian Scholars Conference 8, March 15–16, 2002, Ludwig Von Mises Institute, Auburn University, Auburn, Alabama; http://www.mises.org/pdf/asc/2002/asc8-ritenour.pdf). See also Janet Duitsman Cornelius, *Slave Missions and The Black Church in the Antebellum South* (Columbia, S.C.: University of South Carolina Press, 1999), *passim*.

her to have sexual relations with him, despite her desire not to do so. Rape made Lydia feel guilty and she refused to take communion and, finally, came to Manly for help. At first, he took a hard-line stance with her, telling her to beg her master to stop and saying that he was sure that she could put a stop to it if she tried. In the end, when the rape continued, he softened his approach and agreed not to make it an issue for church discipline. When her master died, Manly bought her and brought her into his own family, making her the nurse over his children.[12]

He also owned slaves, and this practice further shaped his views of the institution. Some slaves became valued members of his family, while others he treated quite differently. Despite preaching many sermons about the duties of masters to make slavery a Christian institution in which slaves were treated humanely and were given religious instruction, and despite admonishing his audience never to break up slave families, he sometimes exposed himself to charges of hypocrisy. One such case in Charleston involved a slave named Claiborne, a young man who became involved in open sin and defiant behavior. After repeated attempts to reform the slave and after numerous whippings, Manly gave up on him and sold him, breaking up the slave family.[13] Not long after, Manly traveled to the north and, in the course of a conversation with another minister on the subject of slavery, told the story of selling Claiborne. When the Northern Baptist

---

12. Fuller, *Chaplain to the Confederacy*, 72–74.

13. "Basil Manly, Sr., Diary II, (1834–1846)," p. 64 (March 1, 1836), Manly Family Papers.

expressed surprise and asked about the sale of slaves, Manly told him that he would sell a slave the same as he would a horse. He soon saw the statement printed in abolitionist papers and heard it used on many occasions by the opponents of slavery. When a Northern minister used the story as a means to oppose Manly's candidacy for an office on the national missions board in 1844, the Southerner felt that his honor had been slighted and moved to defend himself.[14] Out of this personal situation came his strident defense of slavery against Northern Baptists who called it a sin, came Manly's leadership in moving towards a sectional schism, and came the creation of the Southern Baptist Convention.[15]

Basil Manly based his views on slavery on his conception of the Christian family. Here, again, it is too easy simply to label his views as "patriarchal." To be sure, he strongly supported a patriarchal family structure that included slaves as well as women and children, and he expressed the paternalism inherent in such a traditional system of social relations. But he tempered this view with affection and biblical principles that gave women and children informal power within their submissive roles under the husband or father's direction and urged masters to make slavery a Christian institution. Manly's letters to his wife clearly reflect the ways in which he mingled modern notions about affectionate marriage with traditional patriarchy. He and Sarah modeled a much more

14. Basil Manly, Sr., to Basil Manly, Jr., August 26, 1844, Manly Family Papers. See below, pages 109–114.

15. Fuller, *Chaplain to the Confederacy*, 219–224.

complex kind of marriage than simple labels can capture. Sarah obviously exercised informal power in the family, and Basil consulted her on all sorts of matters, both public and private. While he worked as a public man, she often ran the household and also contributed to his work through her active role in the church.[16]

He and Sarah had eight children, six of whom grew to adulthood. The oldest, Basil, Jr., grew to become a close friend, confidant, and fellow minister. Manly trusted his son completely and often poured out his heart to him in his letters. His third child, Charles, also became a preacher, and Manly's correspondence with him came to parallel that with Basil, Jr. Daughters Sarah and Abby and younger sons James and Fuller remained closer to home, but they, too, received their share of letters from their parents. Manly offered fatherly advice, stern warnings about a whole variety of dangers and temptations, as well as all of the news he could pass along. While his diaries indicate a stern discipline over the children, his journals and letters also display a home filled with affection and parental attention. Even though his work demanded his energies, Manly found time to be involved with his children's upbringing.

If the joys of family life reflected God's mercy, Manly could also see judgment in the loss of children. While living in Charleston, the family lost two sons within the space of a year and a half. Little Zebulon Rudulph Manly

16. For a study of Manly's letters to Sarah, see Jonathan A. Lindsey, "Basil Manly: Letters to His Wife," *Quarterly Review*, 35 (1974): 73–84.

died just shy of his second birthday in 1829, and John Waldo Manly expired in November of the following year. Manly's diaries record his grief and the touching scene of three-year-old Basil, Jr., asking for his brother after Rudulph passed away. Manly's sermons on grief after the loss of his children remain powerful statements of how he relied on God in times of trial. Surely, these were times when his piety was played out in the reality of life.[17]

His funeral sermon for John Waldo became an important turning point in Southern Baptist history. In the congregation that day sat Mrs. Ker Boyce, the wife of a wealthy cotton factor and banker. The sermon led to her conversion and she joined Manly's church. Her son, James Petigru Boyce (1827–1888), thus became one of Manly's parishioners. Boyce went on to a brilliant career as a minister, theologian, and one of the key founders of the Southern Baptist Theological Seminary, along with Manly's son, Basil, Jr. He also put his family fortune into the denomination's efforts. Thus, even an event that might be called judgment could lead to divine mercy.[18]

Among his family concerns, Manly paid careful attention to the education of his children. All of them received the best instruction the family could provide and afford. After starting their education at home, sons went to private schools, then to college and seminary. Daughters also received home schooling and private school. His emphasis on learning pervaded Manly's thought, and he worked

---

17. See below, pages 75–81.
18. Fuller, *Chaplain to the Confederacy*, esp. 228–253. For more details, see below, page 81.

hard for educational efforts. In 1830, he undertook work
to support the theological school at the Furman Academy.
He began calling for South-wide cooperation to support a
Baptist theological institution at that time and, when the
effort at Furman failed, he renewed his public plea for a
southern Baptist theological seminary. His work did not
bear fruit for many long years, but eventually his vision
passed to a new generation and he helped them found the
Southern Baptist Theological Seminary in 1859.[19]

The University of Alabama

Education took Manly from Charleston and South Carolina in 1837 when he became president of the University
of Alabama. He moved to Tuscaloosa, where he restored
discipline, expanded the school's curriculum, modern-
ized its facilities, and oversaw a period of expansion and
building. He sought to merge the liberal arts with a classical education while defending both against critics who
wanted to install a more practical curriculum that would
prepare students for work. Living out his faith as a university president raised new challenges for Manly, as he
strove to maintain his position as a gentleman and public man while also promoting the gospel. Once again, he
turned to duty as the means by which to reconcile the
tensions between honor and Christianity.[20]

---

19. Fuller, *Chaplain to the Confederacy*, 78–82. Also see Cecil Clifford,
"The Role of Basil Manly, 1798–1868, in the Establishment of Furman
University and the Southern Baptist Theological Seminary" (master's
thesis, Furman University, 1962).

20. Fuller, *Chaplain to the Confederacy*, 154–181.

The University of Alabama before the Civil War

His new role did not diminish his ministerial work, since his leadership of the university served to expand his influence among Baptists. Although he did not preach as often as he had earlier, Manly still found time to speak in churches, and his leadership of the denomination in the state caused some to call him the "Bishop of Alabama." Sometimes overbearing and tending toward arrogance in his actions, Manly offset such faults with tireless labor and sincere intentions. He involved himself in reform efforts, and his leadership on issues like public education, the treatment of the insane, prison reform, and temperance marked his efforts to fulfill his Christian duty in society at large. His ministry now centered on work for his local church in Tuscaloosa and in reform, but he also spent summers traveling widely across the state as an evangelist. Further, his intellectual abilities and influential position lent themselves to denominational leadership at the national as well as the state level.[21]

His denominational leadership included speaking out on matters of doctrine. Time and again, he defended Calvinist theology. This included working for a number of years with Basil, Jr., to compile a new hymnal. Published in 1850, The *Baptist Psalmody* delivered a collection of hymns that were sound on Calvinist doctrine. Manly loved music, played the violin, and had defended the use of instruments in the church while serving at First Baptist in Charleston. Music played too important a role for ministers to neglect it theologically. Manly's most famous

21. Fuller, *Chaplain to the Confederacy*, 182–211.

theological sermon came in 1849 in the form of "Divine Efficiency Consistent with Human Activity."[22] Delivered at a time when the Arminian doctrine of free will seemed to be advancing among many Baptists, the sermon couched a strict defense of Calvinism and its doctrines of grace and election in gentle terms of reconciliation. Throughout his career, Manly concerned himself more with the practical side of the ministry than with theology. Still, he remained a strict Calvinist, and his sermons and style strongly defended that position. Especially significant in a time of widespread revival, his theological views illustrated Manly's intellectual abilities. In theology, he walked a fine line between those who would throw off doctrine for the sake of popularity and church growth and those who would be so legalistic that their religion would become stagnant. Thus, while still strictly Calvinist, Manly allowed for revivals and interdenominational cooperation.[23]

Manly also spoke out on other issues. His reform efforts included support for the Sunday School movement, and he pushed for the organization of classes in Baptist churches. He also founded the Alabama State Historical Society in 1850. Economics always attracted attention. He bought a plantation near Tuscaloosa and became a planter. While

---

22. For excerpts from this sermon, see below, pages 115–125.

23. Fuller, *Chaplain to the Confederacy*, 94–95, 210–211. For more on Manly's theology, see Tom Nettles, *The Baptists: Key People Involved in Forming a Baptist Identity* (Fearn, Ross-shire: Mentor/Christian Focus, 2005), 2:250–284. In *Chaplain to the Confederacy*, I mistakenly identified Manly as a "General Baptist" early in the book. I correctly labeled him a "strict Calvinist" later in the biography. I apologetically note the error here.

also supporting economic diversification and investment in industry, he sought to improve Southern agriculture through science and education and helped organize the state agricultural society. He often spoke of Christian economics in his sermons, where he noted the duty associated with prosperity and balanced the capitalistic desire for profit with biblical standards for managing wealth.[24]

Economic crisis served as the context for one of Manly's most important statements on politics and slavery. The state bank of Alabama failed in 1844. During the resulting crisis, Manly delivered a sermon before an interdenominational audience on a fast day called for by the governor. "National Stability" not only featured a states' rights Democrat's views on banks and debt, it also contained his thoughts about immigration and an appeal for ameliorating the evils of slavery with Christianity. Manly called for missionary work among the slaves and argued that Christian masters must fulfill their duty in bringing the gospel to those in bondage. Some historians argue that appeals to reform slavery like this one were an inherent threat to the peculiar institution, although Manly remained staunchly pro-slavery and defended the institution more vigorously as the years went by.[25]

His actions as a master revealed the complexities of

24. Fuller, *Chaplain to the Confederacy*, 146, 254–267.

25. Fuller, *Chaplain to the Confederacy*, 212–216. For an example of historians' seeing the Christian call for amelioration as a threat to slavery, see Eugene D. Genovese, *A Consuming Fire: The Fall of the Confederacy in the Mind of the White Christian South* (Athens: University of Georgia Press, 1998), 1–33.

slavery and again exposed him to charges of hypocrisy. In 1846, he whipped a slave owned by the University of Alabama for insolence. The beating took place in front of the faculty, and when Manly thought the slave, a man named Sam, was not properly humbled, he whipped him a second time, more severely. The Baptist preacher thought his honor had been slighted, and his actions reflected the way he responded to the perceived insult. Such incidents lent credence to charges of cruelty made against him. The wife of John L. Dagg (1794–1884), a fellow Baptist minister and educator who later served as president of Mercer University, charged that Manly regularly beat his slaves just for exercise![26] When this was repeated as one of the reasons not to elect him to a national missions board in 1844, Manly scrambled to find the source of the story and began working harder than ever for the separation of the Southern Baptists from the national conventions. For him, the sectional schism and creation of the Southern Baptist Convention was a matter of personal honor as well as principle.[27]

Chaplain to the Confederate government

In 1855, Manly resigned his position as president of the University of Alabama and accepted a call to preach at the Wentworth Street Baptist Church in Charleston, South Carolina. After so many years in Alabama, Manly wondered, "What is the Lord carrying me to Charleston

---

26. See below, pages 109–114.
27. Fuller, *Chaplain to the Confederacy*, 216–224.

The President's Mansion at the University
of Alabama before the Civil War

for?" His reputation and influence in Alabama made leaving the state difficult. With his family well-situated, a plantation to run, and many duties to fulfill, he struggled with the decision. In the end, he felt that God wanted him to go to Charleston, and so he went. While there, he threw himself into his ministerial duties, continued to work on behalf of reform, and maintained his leadership in the denomination. Some might judge his decision to go back to Charleston a mistake. While his ministry did result in some conversions and he continued many of his previous activities, the most significant events during his tenure at the church were the stealing of church funds by an embezzler and the yellow fever epidemic of 1858. But Manly trusted in God's planning rather than his own. His second tenure in Charleston was short, and he resigned in December of 1858 and returned to Alabama.[28]

There he first took a position as an evangelist, then accepted the call to serve as pastor at the First Baptist Church of Montgomery in 1860. While there, he served as official chaplain to the provisional government of the Confederacy. Manly saw the new Confederate States of America as the fulfillment of his long-held dream for a separate Southern nation, and he called on God to bless the government and its actions. His most significant public prayer on behalf of the Confederacy came on February 18, 1861, when he served as chaplain for the inauguration of Confederate President Jefferson Davis (1808–1889).[29]

---

28. Fuller, *Chaplain to the Confederacy*, 268–286.
29. See below, pages 127–130.

The Civil War soon shaped a new context for his life as he continued his ministerial duties in Montgomery until the end of 1862. Declining health and concerns for his family and property led him to resign his post and move back home to Tuscaloosa. When the war turned against the South, he struggled to hold on to his faith in both God and the Confederacy. His two youngest sons, James and Fuller, served in the Confederate military, and Manly himself worked tirelessly on the home front. The defeat of the South brought crisis and, despite his best efforts, Manly found that he was unable to keep his plantation, which he sold in 1866.

By now, his health had declined. He suffered a stroke in 1864 and, although he continued to preach as much as he could, he had to limit his activities. In 1867, with the plantation sold and his health slipping, he received news that Basil, Jr.'s wife had died. That left his son with eight children to care for even as he worked as a professor at the Southern Baptist Theological Seminary in Greenville, South Carolina. So Manly and his wife moved there to help Basil, Jr., and his family. In his last months, he wrote letters to keep the scattered members of his family together through correspondence, and he served as a trusted advisor to the seminary's leaders. Manly still continued to preach and often spoke to the seminary students. His last sermon came just three weeks before his death on December 21, 1868.[30]

Basil Manly died secure in his faith and trusting in

---

30. Fuller, *Chaplain to the Confederacy*, 286–315.

Jesus Christ as his Lord and Savior. Throughout his life and career, he had seen both God's mercy and God's judgment, and he had experienced both success and failure. He had reconciled mercy and judgment and brought together faith and honor, all in the concept of duty. Mercy and success had come in the blessings of revival, in the attainment of social status and influence, in economic wealth, in the prosperity of his family, in the richness of close friendships, and in the fulfillment of long-held dreams. Judgment and failure had been manifested in times of trouble and trial, in the breaking of the bonds of friendship, in the loss of property, the death of family members and friends, and in the defeat of the Confederacy. Through it all, Basil Manly lived out his faith, as piety pervaded every aspect of his life. Economics, church issues, politics, education, family matters, slavery—Manly viewed and interpreted these and other issues in light of his faith. In his life, piety came in the experience of both mercy and judgment and their reconciliation in duty. Good and bad, right and wrong, public and private, success and failure, all came together in Christian duty. Thus, he could say that life was "a reality indeed" and not a failure and that "taking up Jesus as the aim of life" was "sufficient to support a man" and that he would be "willing, with Him, to live life over" again.

Basil Manly, Jr.

"Soldiers of Christ, in truth arrayed":
The ministry and piety of Basil Manly, Jr. (1825–1892)
by Michael A. G. Haykin

A year or so after the death of Basil Manly, Jr., his long-time friend and seminary colleague John A. Broadus (1827–1895) expressed the hope that a memoir of Manly would soon appear.[1] Nothing of substance was written by any who knew Manly, though, beyond a few brief pieces in a special edition of the *Seminary Magazine* and an article by John R. Sampey (1863–1948), Southern's fifth seminary president, in a 1908 issue of the *Review and Expositor*.[2] Thus, while there are extensive memoirs of both of Manly's long-standing seminary colleagues, James Petigru Boyce (1827–1888) and John Broadus, by men who knew them well, no such study exists that covers Manly's theology,

1. *Memoir of James Petigru Boyce, D.D., LL.D.* (New York: A. C. Armstrong and Son, 1893), 326 n. 2. There were hopes that Sampey would produce a biographical memoir of Manly, but it was not to be. See James M. Manley, "The Southern Baptist Mind in Transition: A Life of Basil Manly, Jr., 1825–1892" (Ph.D. dissertation, University of Florida, 1999), 291 n. 77.

2. *Seminary Magazine*, 5, no. 6 (March 1892); John R. Sampey, "B. Manly, Jr.," *Review and Expositor*, 5, no. 3 (July, 1908): 405–418.

piety, public ministry and private family life.[3] Nor did Manly leave behind a large literary legacy. Apart from a substantial study of the doctrine of inspiration,[4] there are, in the words of A. T. Robertson (1863–1934), only a few "fugitive articles in newspapers and magazines, occasional addresses and pamphlets."[5]

Yet, in the last fifty-five years or so, two excellent biographical studies of Manly have appeared—both of them doctoral theses—as well as an important doctoral study of his hymnological significance.[6] Moreover, despite the

---

3. For Boyce, see Broadus, *Memoir of James Petigru Boyce*, and for Broadus, see A. T. Robertson, *Life and Letters of John Albert Broadus* (Philadelphia: American Baptist Publication Society, 1901). For contemporary studies, see especially David S. Dockery and Roger D. Duke, eds., *John A. Broadus: A Living Legacy*, Studies in Baptist Life and Thought (Nashville: B & H Publishing, 2008) and Thomas J. Nettles, *James Petigru Boyce*, American Reformed Biographies (Phillipsburg, N.J.: P&R Publishing Company, 2009).

4. *The Bible Doctrine of Inspiration Explained and Vindicated* (1888; repr., Harrisonburg, Va.: Gano Books / Sprinkle Publications, 1985).

5. "Rev. Basil Manly, D.D., LL.D.," *Seminary Magazine*, 5, no. 6 (March 1892): 297.

6. Joseph Powhatan Cox, "A Study of the Life and Work of Basil Manly, Jr." (Th.D. thesis, Southern Baptist Theological Seminary, 1954); Manley, "Southern Baptist Mind in Transition"; Nathan Harold Platt, "The Hymnological Contributions of Basil Manly Jr. to the Congregational Song of Southern Baptists" (D.M.A. dissertation, Southern Baptist Theological Seminary, 2004). For a concise biographical study, see also Gregory A. Wills, "Manly, Basil, Jr.," *American National Biography* (New York and Oxford: Oxford University Press, 1999), 14:417–418.

It will be evident that the biographical section of this article relies significantly on Manley's study. As such, it must be noted that Manley makes much of the fact that throughout his life Basil Manly was subject to episodes of depression, episodes that were particularly crippling in his early years (see especially "Southern Baptist Mind in Transition," 8, 10–12, 29–30, 37–38, 66–72, 76–81, 107–112, 294 ["melancholy" was

fact that Manly left relatively little by way of a written corpus, there are two public texts associated with Southern Seminary that come directly from his hand—the seminary's statement of faith and the seminary hymn—and both have exercised a profound influence on Southern Baptist life. If the right questions be asked, they reveal a tremendous amount about Manly's theological and spiritual convictions.

"All my life a stopper of gaps": A sketch of Manly's life[7]

Basil Manly, Jr., was the eldest son of one of the most prominent antebellum Southern Baptist ministers, Basil Manly, Sr. (1798–1868), who moved to South Carolina shortly after his son's birth to pastor the First Baptist Church of Charleston.[8] The elder Manly was pastor of this congregation from 1826 through 1837, and thus the younger Manly's earliest years were spent in Charleston. It was here that he first met James Petigru Boyce, who became a boyhood friend and whose mother had come to faith in Christ under the elder Manly's ministry in 1830.

"his life's companion"], 303–304). While some might question the importance that Manley places on these episodes in the overall shape of his subject's life, this does not negate, in the opinion of this writer, the overall usefulness of Manley's study.

   7. The quote is from a letter from Manly to his son George Manly, September 28, 1878, Basil Manly Papers, 10:296, James P. Boyce Centennial Library Archives, Southern Baptist Theological Seminary, Louisville, Ky. This collection of letters is henceforth cited as Basil Manly Papers, with the relevant volume and page numbers.

   8. For the elder Manly, see above, pages 1–23.

Manly, Jr., moved to Tuscaloosa, Alabama, in 1837 with his family when his father accepted the presidency of the University of Alabama in August of that year. Three years later the younger Manly entered the freshman class of this university, where he was converted, in large part through the reading of the *Personal Narrative* of the New England divine Jonathan Edwards (1703–1758).[9] He was baptized on October 18, 1840, by his father in the Black Warrior River, which flows past Tuscaloosa. Graduating from the university in December 1843, Manly spent a year of graduate study at Newton Theological Institution, near Boston, Massachusetts, from 1844 to 1845. Though a Baptist school, the theological and spiritual climate was far too tepid for Manly's liking.[10] When the Southern Baptist Convention was formed in 1845, an event in which his father played a key role,[11] Manly transferred to Princeton, where he studied under what has been well described as "perhaps the finest theological faculty in the United States."[12]

9. Manley, "Southern Baptist Mind in Transition," 20–21.

10. Manley, "Southern Baptist Mind in Transition," 43–60.

11. Michael Sugrue, "'We Desired Our Future Rulers to Be Educated Men': South Carolina College, the Defense of Slavery, and the Development of Secessionist Politics" in *The American College in the Nineteenth Century*, ed. Roger L. Geiger (Nashville: Vanderbilt University Press, 2000), 306 n. 103.

12. Manley, "Southern Baptist Mind in Transition," 65. On Princeton, see especially David B. Calhoun, *Princeton Seminary*, 2 vols. (Edinburgh and Carlisle, Pa.: Banner of Truth Trust, 1994, 1996). For Manly's time at Princeton, see Manley, "Southern Baptist Mind in Transition," 59–82. Of all his teachers at Princeton, Manly believed that he learned the most from Charles Hodge (1797–1878). See Broadus, *Memoir of James Petigru Boyce*, 73.

After graduation from Princeton in 1847 with a diploma in theological studies, Manly spent roughly fifteen months, from January 1848 to March 1849, pastoring three rural churches, two in Alabama and one close by in Mississippi. There is the distinct possibility that he pastored the three works simultaneously, since, like most rural or village churches of the time, they probably had preaching services but once or twice a month.[13] Nevertheless, Manly experienced a breakdown in his health and he ended up leaving all three churches in early 1849. The rest of that year was taken up to some degree with the compilation, with his father's help, of a hymnal, *The Baptist Psalmody* (1850).[14] In 1850 he accepted a call to the prestigious First Baptist Church of Richmond, Virginia, where he labored until 1854, when he resigned to take up the presidency of the Richmond Female Institute.[15]

It was during these years in Richmond that Manly became a keen supporter of the establishment of Sunday Schools, a concern that eventually led to his being elected president of the first Southern Baptist Sunday School Board in May of 1863,[16] and his frequent writ-

---

13. Joseph Powhatan Cox, "Manly, Basil, Jr.," *Encyclopedia of Southern Baptists* (Nashville: Broadman Press, 1958), 2:818; Manley, "Southern Baptist Mind in Transition," 83–88.

14. For some of Manly's hymns from this hymnal, see below, pages 133–137.

15. For Manly's time in Richmond, see Manley, "Southern Baptist Mind in Transition," 99–155. For his letter of acceptance, see his letter to the Trustees of the Richm[d.] Female Institute, April 18, 1854, Basil Manly Papers, vol. 1.

16. William A. Mueller, *A History of Southern Baptist Theological Seminary* (Nashville: Broadman Press, 1959), 92–93.

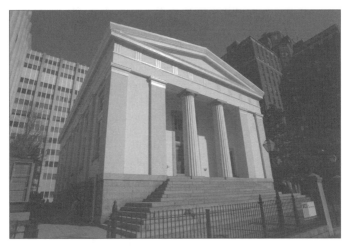

Old building of First Baptist Church of Richmond, Virginia, now used as the Virginia Commonwealth University's Hunton Student Center on the Medical College of Virginia Campus

(Photo: Win Grant)

ing of Sunday School material for children over the next three decades.[17] In June 1852 he preached a sermon to a gathering of Virginia Baptists, the title of which became part of a well-known motto: "A Sunday School in Every Baptist Church."[18] Central to Manly's argumentation was that Sunday Schools were designed to impart knowledge of the Scriptures and theology to both children and adults. "Religious knowledge is essential to true piety," he emphasized, and though the former cannot produce the latter, "there is no true religion without knowledge."[19]

In 1859 Manly entered what "he considered his life's great work"—his professorship at Southern.[20] Manly's commitment to theological education can be gauged by words he had written three years earlier, when he stated that the "cause of theological education is one dearer to me than almost any other and I esteem no sacrifice too great for its promotion."[21] One of the four founding faculty,

---

17. See, for example, the preface to his *Little Lessons for Little People. Number I* (Greenville, S.C.: Sunday School Board Southern Baptist Convention, 1864), in which he told his young readers, "This little book has been made especially for you, by one who loves children." For more details of this aspect of Manly's life, see Sampey, "B. Manly, Jr.," 407–409; Manley, "Southern Baptist Mind in Transition," 190–196.

18. *Baptist Preacher*, 11 (1852): 117–136. This sermon is reproduced in H. Leon McBeth, *A Sourcebook for Baptist Heritage* (Nashville: Broadman Press, 1990), 291–295. The motto that Manly used later in life was "A Sunday School in Every Baptist Church and Every Baptist in the Sunday School" (Sampey, "B. Manly, Jr.," 407).

19. *Baptist Preacher*, 128.

20. The quote is from Wills, "Manly, Basil, Jr.," 418.

21. Basil Manly, Jr., to John B. O'Neall, September 13, 1856, Manly Collection of Manuscripts, folder 64, microfilm reel 1, Southern Baptist Theological Seminary Archives). Quoted in Gregory A. Wills, *Southern*

Manly was assigned the task of teaching the Old Testament and Hebrew.[22] His work in this regard was halted by
the Civil War when the seminary had to close from 1862
to 1865. Then, six years after the resumption of seminary
life, Manly decided to accept the offer of the presidency
of Georgetown College in Kentucky. Key reasons induc-
ing Manly to move to Kentucky were the opportunity
he would have personally to supervise the education of
his children, his deep distaste for the postwar politics of
South Carolina, a better salary, and a dislike for correcting
written sermons in his class on homiletics, something he
had come to regard as sheer "drudgery."[23] It is noteworthy
that during his tenure at Georgetown from 1871 to 1879,[24]
Manly experienced deep regrets about leaving the seminary. As he wrote to Broadus in 1875, "I loved that work,
and the men that were associated with me in it, as I never
expect to love any other. And probably I ought to have
clung to it to the end, through thick and thin."[25]

Baptist Theological Seminary, 1859–2009 (New York: Oxford University
Press, forthcoming), chapter 1.

22. Manley, "Southern Baptist Mind in Transition," 142–143,
163–164, 197. During his career at Southern, on occasion he also taught
Greek, biblical introduction, homiletics, Assyrian, and apologetics
(Manley, "Southern Baptist Mind in Transition," 164–165, 197; Wills,
"Manly, Basil, Jr.," 418). For details of his teaching the Old Testament,
see Mueller, *History of Southern Baptist Theological Seminary*, 90–91.

23. Broadus, *Memoir of James Petigru Boyce*, 214; Manley, "Southern
Baptist Mind in Transition," 215–216; Wills, "Manly, Basil, Jr.," 418.

24. For this period in his life, see Manley, "Southern Baptist Mind
in Transition," 219–242.

25. Basil Manly, Jr., to John A. Broadus, April 28, 1875, Broadus
Papers, box 6, James P. Boyce Centennial Library Archives, Southern

During the time Manly was in Georgetown, the seminary also relocated to Kentucky, namely, to Louisville in 1877. And it was also during this period of time that Crawford H. Toy (1836–1919), who joined the faculty in 1869 and who took over Manly's teaching in the Old Testament, was compelled to leave the seminary after controversy erupted over his adoption of a critical methodology that denied the facticity of some of the historical, geographical, and geological assertions of the Old Testament.[26] Within days of Toy's departure in the spring of 1879, Manly was re-elected to the faculty as Professor of Old Testament.[27] That fall as Manly began teaching once again at the seminary, he delivered a public lecture, "Why and How to Study the Bible," in which he made clear his position vis-à-vis the Toy Controversy. Toy was not men-

Baptist Theological Seminary, Louisville, Ky. Cited in Wills, *Southern Baptist Theological Seminary*, chapter 2.

26. For a clear statement of Toy's position, see his letter of resignation from the faculty in Robert A. Baker, ed., *A Baptist Source Book, With Particular Reference to Southern Baptists* (Nashville: Broadman Press, 1966), 168–172. For two helpful overviews of the Toy controversy, see Timothy George, introduction to *The Bible Doctrine of Inspiration*, by Basil Manly, Jr. (Nashville: Broadman & Holman, 1995), 6–9; and Jeffrey Paul Straub, "The Making of a Battle Royal: The Rise of Religious Liberalism in Northern Baptist Life, 1870–1920" (Ph.D. dissertation, Southern Baptist Theological Seminary, 2004), 72–92. For a sympathetic perspective on Toy, see Mueller, *History of Southern Baptist Theological Seminary*, 135–142.

At the time that Toy joined the faculty, Manly believed that Toy's "attainments…are really remarkable," and that he gave promise of being "valuable not only to our Seminary, & country, but the world" (Basil Manly, Jr., to Adiel Sherwood, December 24, 1869, Basil Manly Papers, 3:246).

27. Manley, "Southern Baptist Mind in Transition," 252.

tioned by Manly in the lecture, but the latter was clearly refuting his views when he asserted that the Bible was "God's words" and "God's truth," "heaven-sent" "sacred oracles" that were distinguished above all by plenary inspiration.[28] As such, Manly forthrightly declared that he was not at all afraid of "being charged with bibliolatry in giving the Bible the central, dominant place in our system and in our affections."[29]

The subject of the inspiration of the Scriptures continued to occupy Manly's mind and theological research throughout the 1880s, eventuating in *The Bible Doctrine of Inspiration Explained and Vindicated* (1888), a comprehensive scholarly argument for the position that "the Bible as a whole is the Word of God, so that in every part of Scripture there is both infallible truth and divine authority."[30] Manly had written the book during the summer of 1887 when he and his wife had a prolonged vacation at a farmhouse near Asheville, North Carolina.[31]

In December 1888, his old friend and seminary col-

---

28. Manley, "Southern Baptist Mind in Transition," 256. For other summaries of this lecture, see George, introduction to *Bible Doctrine of Inspiration*, 9–10; L. Russ Bush and Tom J. Nettles, *Baptists and the Bible*, rev. ed. (Nashville: Broadman & Holman, 1999), 190–191.

29. Cited in George, introduction to *Bible Doctrine of Inspiration*, 10.

30. *Bible Doctrine of Inspiration*, 59. Basil's younger brother Charles Manly (1837–1924) played a significant role in encouraging Basil to write this book. See Manley, "Southern Baptist Mind in Transition," 263–264. For summaries of the book, see Manley, "Southern Baptist Mind in Transition," 264–269; Bush and Nettles, *Baptists and the Bible*, 191–196. For extracts, see below, pages 197–201.

31. Basil Manly, Jr., to A. H. Newman, April 23, [1888], Basil Manly Papers, 19:315–316.

league Boyce died on a trip to Europe and was succeeded as seminary president by Broadus. The latter knew the seminary's great need of Manly's scholarship, piety, and versatility — Manly once referred to himself as a "stopper of gaps," though Broadus preferred to regard him as "the most versatile man" he had ever known.[32] Broadus thus wrote to him a month after Boyce's death to tell him that he valued his "advice in Seminary matters beyond that of all other men." He and Manly must therefore "husband [their] strength, and stand together, like two old oxen."[33] Manly continued to serve faithfully at the seminary as his strength allowed until his death on January 31, 1892.[34] Many of Manly's Baptist contemporaries found it striking that this was the very same day that the English Baptist preacher, C. H. Spurgeon (1834–1892), died in France.

One of the "brightest intellectual stars" of his generation,[35] Manly must be remembered as a central figure in the establishment, shaping, and preservation of what would become his denomination's flagship seminary. Along with Boyce and Broadus, he consciously sought to make Southern a place where a profound interface of intellect and piety could occur.[36] And as the two texts that remain cen-

---

32. Basil Manly, Jr., to George Manly, September 28, 1878, in Robertson, *Life and Letters of John Albert Broadus*, 399. On the value of Manly's versatility, see also Cox, "Manly, Basil, Jr.," 818; Wills, "Manly, Basil, Jr.," 418.

33. Broadus to Basil Manly, Jr., January 28, 1889, in Robertson, *Life and Letters of John Albert Broadus*, 374.

34. For Manly's final days, see Manley, "Southern Baptist Mind in Transition," 290–292.

35. Manley, "Southern Baptist Mind in Transition," 302.

36. Timothy George traces this interface to the influence of Prince-

tral to the legacy of that founding generation bear witness, he — and his colleagues — succeeded admirably.

Writing a "creed": Manly and the Abstract of Principles [37]

The Abstract of Principles, the seminary's statement of faith, was drawn up by Manly in the months of March and April 1858[38] and was based on the classical Calvinistic Baptist confession of the seventeenth century — the Second London Confession of Faith (1677/1689).[39] When Manly originally began work on what became the Abstract of Principles, he told his younger brother Charles Manly (1837–1924) that he hoped to use both this seventeenth-century confession and the first Calvinistic Baptist statement, the First London Confession of Faith (1644; 2nd ed., 1646), as its basis.[40] As it turned out, though, Manly

tonian Christianity on Boyce and Manly (introduction to *Bible Doctrine of Inspiration*, 3–4, 5, and 13 n. 7). But it would also have been modeled in the life of Manly's father, who played a critical role in both Boyce's and his son's lives.

37. Manly called the future Abstract of Principles a "creed" in his letter to John A. Broadus, February 15, 1858 (Robertson, *Life and Letters of John Albert Broadus*, 146–147).

38. On April 20, 1858, Manly wrote to his brother Charles Manly, "I finished my Confession of Faith last night, and sent it off to Boyce" (Basil Manly Papers, 1842–1893 [ms. 486-z], Southern Historical Collection, University of North Carolina at Chapel Hill, henceforth abbreviated as BMSHC). Cited in Manley, "Southern Baptist Mind in Transition," 163 n. 18. See also the discussion by Cox, "Life and Work of Basil Manly, Jr.," 145–151.

39. Wills, "Manly, Basil, Jr.," 418.

40. Basil Manly, Jr., to Charles Manly, March 1, 1858 (BMSHC). Greg Wills points out that this letter was written to Manly's brother,

produced an abridgement of only the 1689 Confession, which had been very familiar to him from his youth.[41]

As noted above, the younger Manly had spent his earliest years immersed in what some later historians have referred to as the "Charleston Tradition."[42] Between the founding of the First Baptist Church of Charleston and the middle of the eighteenth century, this congregation helped in the organization of four more churches that came to constitute the Charleston Association in 1751. Sixteen years later this association took virtually all of the Philadelphia Confession of Faith (1742) — essentially a reproduction of the Second London Confession, with the addition of an article on the laying on of hands and also one on the singing of psalms, hymns, and spiritual songs — for its statement of doctrinal convictions. The sole area of difference was the Charleston confession's omission of the article on the laying on of hands. The 1767 Charleston confession was reprinted in 1813, 1831, and 1850, clear indication that it was a vital document for the churches of this association and that the younger Manly would have definitely been acquainted with it.[43]

---

and not Boyce, as Cox had argued ("Life and Work of Basil Manly, Jr.," 146). See Wills, *Southern Baptist Theological Seminary*, chapter 1.

41. Manley, "Southern Baptist Mind in Transition," 160. Timothy George mistakenly includes the First London Confession along with the 1689 Confession as a basis for the Abstract of Principles (introduction to *Bible Doctrine of Inspiration*, 4).

42. Manley, "Southern Baptist Mind in Transition," 16.

43. James Leo Garrett, Jr., *Baptist Church Discipline* (Nashville: Broadman Press, 1962), 16; William L. Lumpkin, *Baptist Confessions of Faith*, rev. ed. (Valley Forge, Pa.: Judson Press, 1969), 352.

There is little doubt that the Abstract of Principles contains a robust expression of the Calvinistic soteriology of the Charleston tradition in which Manly had been raised and which he had come to embrace wholeheartedly.[44] In only one key area of the perspective of the Charleston tradition on salvation did Manly leave room for significant difference of opinion — namely, the doctrine of particular redemption. Instead of the forthright statement of the Second London Confession that to "all those for whom Christ hath obtained eternal redemption, he doth certainly, and effectually apply and communicate the same," the Abstract of Principles simply states that Jesus Christ "suffered and died upon the cross for the salvation of sinners."[45] Particular redemption had been a flashpoint of controversy not only between Calvinists and Arminians in the nineteenth century, but also within the ranks of Calvinistic Baptists.[46] Manly clearly intended that those who held to various perspectives on particular

44. Abstract of Principles V–XIII. For this statement of faith, see below, pages 145–150.

45. Second London Confession of Faith VIII.8 (Lumpkin, *Baptist Confessions of Faith*, 262); Abstract of Principles VII.

46. The clash in Calvinistic circles was between those who followed the view of John Gill (1697–1771), who were known as Gillites, and those who adhered to the perspective of Andrew Fuller (1754–1815), who were called Fullerites. While Gill was a firm believer in the idea that Christ died for the exact number of sins of the elect, Fuller argued that "the sufferings of Christ, in themselves considered, are of infinite value, sufficient to have saved all the world, and a thousand worlds, if it had pleased God to have constituted them the price of their redemption, and to have made them effectual to that end" (*A Defence of a Treatise entitled The Gospel Worthy of All Acceptation containing A Reply to Mr. Button's Remarks and the Observations of Philanthropos*, in *The Complete Works*

redemption and those who affirmed a general redemption
could sign their agreement to this statement.[47]

Yet, a close reading of the clause in the Abstract of
Principles that immediately follows the one cited above
provides a hint regarding Manly's convictions about the
atonement. There it is affirmed that Christ "ever liveth to
make intercession for His people."[48] The biblical support
for the specificity of the ascended Lord's prayers, namely,
"for his people," can be found in passages like John 17:9.
To the majority of Manly's Calvinistic Baptist forebears
and contemporaries, such specificity in prayer implied a
particularity with regard to the death of Christ. John Gill
(1697–1771), the English Baptist theologian whose views
were considered oracular by many even down to Manly's
day,[49] put it succinctly when he stated in his commentary
on John 17:9: "for whom [Christ] is the propitiation, he

---

of the Rev. Andrew Fuller, ed. Joseph Belcher [1845; repr., Harrisonburg,
Va.: Sprinkle Publications, 1988], 2:488–489).

    See, for example, David Benedict, *Fifty Years Among the Baptists*
(New York: Sheldon, 1860), 135–144; James Petigru Boyce, *Abstract of
Systematic Theology* (1887; repr., Cape Coral, Fl.: Founders Press, 2006),
311–335; Anthony L. Chute, *A Piety above the Common Standard: Jesse Mercer
and the Defense of Evangelistic Calvinism* (Macon, Ga.: Mercer University
Press, 2004), *passim*; Jarrett Burch, *Adiel Sherwood: Baptist Antebellum Pioneer in Georgia* (Macon, Ga.: Mercer University Press, 2003), 90–92,
242–243.

    47. Manley, "Southern Baptist Mind in Transition," 162.

    48. Abstract of Principles VII.

    49. See, for example, the preface to the Charleston Association's
A Summary of Church Discipline (1774) — reprinted in 1794, 1813, 1831, and
1850 — in which the authors acknowledged being "greatly indebted to
the late learned, pious, and judicious Dr. Gill" (Garrett, *Baptist Church
Discipline*, 27–28). See also above, n. 47.

is an advocate; and for whom he died, he makes intercession."[50] Gill regarded the idea of Christ's not praying for
all of those for whom He died as "absurd and incredible."[51]
Similarly, Manly's colleague Boyce argued that Christ's
priestly work in heaven involves intercession "with God
for pardon or justification or other blessings for all for
whom He died, in all the respects in which His death is
available for each."[52]

A second public text left by Manly, which contains a
rich expression of his piety, is Southern Seminary's hymn.

"Let all the people praise God": Manly as hymnwriter and hymnologist [53]

Manly had grown up in a home where music was a central
feature of the family's life. His father had given him and

---

50. *Exposition of the New Testament* (London, 1809; repr., Paris, Ark.:
Baptist Standard Bearer, 1989), 2:86.

51. *A Complete Body of Doctrinal and Practical Divinity*, book VI, chap.
III (1839; repr., Paris, Ark.: Baptist Standard Bearer, 1989), 466.

52. *Abstract of Systematic Theology*, 293. For a concise overview of the
Calvinism of the founding faculty of Southern and Broadus's appar-
ent commitment to particular redemption, see Wills, *Southern Baptist
Theological Seminary*, chapter 2. On the contemporary significance of the
Abstract of Principles for Southern Seminary, see R. Albert Mohler,
Jr., "Don't just do something, stand there! Southern Seminary and the
Abstract of Principles," *Southern Seminary Magazine*, 68, no. 4 (November
2000): 2–5. This article was first given as a convocation address at the
Southern Baptist Theological Seminary, August 31, 1993, and can also
be found at http://www.albertmohler.com/documents/TwoInaugu-
ralAddresses.pdf and at http://www.founders.org/stand.html.

53. The quote is from the preface to *The Choice* (1892) and is a
conscious echo of Psalm 67:3, 5. This preface can be found in Platt,
"Hymnological Contributions of Basil Manly Jr.," 216. See below, pages
217–218.

his siblings musical instruction, and both he and his father played the violin.[54] His father was also deeply versed in hymnody, an interest that bore fruit when he and his son compiled the first hymnbook of the Southern Baptists, *The Baptist Psalmody*, which appeared in 1850.[55] This hymnal well displays the younger Manly's profound love for the classical hymns of the Christian Faith. Three hundred nineteen texts in *The Baptist Psalmody* are by Isaac Watts (1674–1748), the so-called father of English hymnody.[56] Other hymnwriters liberally represented include three of the great hymnwriters of the eighteenth century:[57] Philip Doddridge (1702–1751), Charles Wesley (1707–1788), and John Newton (1725–1807), and the two outstanding Baptist hymnwriters from that same era: Anne Steele (1717–1778) and Benjamin Beddome (1717–1795).[58] This

---

54. Richardson, "Basil Manly, Jr.: Southern Baptist Pioneer in Hymnody," 95–96; Fuller, *Chaplain to the Confederacy*, 94–95.

55. For a study of this hymnal, see Platt, "Hymnological Contributions of Basil Manly Jr.," 42–65. Also see Paul A. Richardson, "Basil Manly, Jr.: Southern Baptist Pioneer in Hymnody," in *Singing Baptists: Studies in Baptist Hymnody in America*, ed. Harry Eskew, David W. Music, and Paul A. Richardson (Nashville: Church Street Press, 1994), 97–101. This chapter is a revised version of the article of the same name that appeared in *Baptist History and Heritage*, 27 (1992): 19–30.

56. Platt, "Hymnological Contributions of Basil Manly Jr.," 46, 190.

57. Seventy-one hymns were by Doddridge, fifty-two by Wesley, and forty-three by Newton (Platt, "Hymnological Contributions of Basil Manly Jr.," 46–47, 190).

58. Richardson, "Basil Manly, Jr.: Southern Baptist Pioneer in Hymnody," 99. Fifty-two hymns were by Steele and forty-six by Beddome (Platt, "Hymnological Contributions of Basil Manly Jr.," 189). For Steele, see the definitive life by J. R. Broome, *A Bruised Reed: Anne Steele: Her Life and Times* (Harpenden, Hertfordshire: Gospel Standard Trust Publications, 2007). For Beddome, see Thomas Brooks, *Pictures of the*

hymnal also contains nine hymns written by Manly, none
of which, in the judgment of Paul Richardson, is "a great
hymn," though "all are polished and meet or surpass the
standard of much hymnody of the time."[59] One of these
hymns, "Holy, holy, holy Lord," was included by C. H.
Spurgeon in the London Metropolitan Tabernacle's *Our
Own Hymn-Book*.[60] According to Manly's own estimate, *The
Baptist Psalmody* was very successful and sold between fifty
and sixty thousand copies over the next twenty-five years
or so.[61]

In 1859, when Manly was in the process of moving to
Greenville, South Carolina, to take up his position at the
brand-new seminary, a "tune and hymn book" he had co-
authored with a well-known Virginian musician by the
name of Asa Brooks Everett (1828–1875) was published.
Although *Baptist Chorals* enjoyed limited success, Nathan
Platt regards it as a significant work, since it "preserved
the hymn texts of the preeminent European evangelicals,
Baptist pioneers, and early American church musicians

Past: The History of the Baptist Church, Bourton-on-the-Water (London: Judd
& Glass, 1861), 21–66, and Derrick Holmes, "The Early Years (1655–
1740) of Bourton-on-the-Water Dissenters who later constituted the
Baptist Church, with special reference to the Ministry of the Reverend
Benjamin Beddome A.M. 1740–1795" (certificate in education disserta-
tion, St Paul's College, Cheltenham, 1969).

59. "Basil Manly, Jr.: Southern Baptist Pioneer in Hymnody," 100.
For the text of the hymns, see Platt, "Hymnological Contributions of
Basil Manly Jr.," 235–240.

60. Manley, "Southern Baptist Mind in Transition," 120 n. 86.

61. Cox, "Life and Work of Basil Manly, Jr.," 79; Wills, "Manly,
Basil, Jr.," 417.

while promoting the works of contemporaneous writers and composers."[62]

The *Baptist Chorals* came at the beginning of Manly's teaching at Southern. Near the close of Manly's ministry at the seminary, in 1891, he produced a third hymnbook, which Manly simply called *Manly's Choice*.[63] The reason for this small hymnal of 254 hymns was that Manly was deeply concerned that "the rage for novelties in singing, especially in our Sunday-schools, has been driving out of use the old, precious, standard hymns." Manly was referring to the use of gospel songs — he did not name any authors or composers in particular, but he would have had in mind such figures as Fanny Crosby (1820–1915) and Ira D. Sankey (1840–1908) — which was usurping the place of historic evangelical hymnody, much of which was increasingly unfamiliar to "the young people of today." Manly was not unequivocally opposed to the use of such songs, but he wanted to ensure that the rich hymnody of the past would continue to inform the worship of Baptist congregations.[64] In order to rectify the situation, Manly

---

62. "Hymnological Contributions of Basil Manly Jr.," 104. For studies of *Baptist Chorals*, see Richardson, "Basil Manly, Jr.: Southern Baptist Pioneer in Hymnody," 101–103; Platt, "Hymnological Contributions of Basil Manly Jr.," 66–104.

63. For studies of *Manly's Choice*, see Richardson, "Basil Manly, Jr.: Southern Baptist Pioneer in Hymnody," 106–108; Platt, "Hymnological Contributions of Basil Manly Jr.," 105–149. *Manly's Choice* was a words-only edition. It was followed in 1892 by *The Choice*, which contained the tunes as well as the words. *The Choice* appeared quite soon after Manly's death.

64. Richardson, "Basil Manly, Jr.: Southern Baptist Pioneer in Hymnody," 107–108. On the growing use of gospel songs in Southern

SOUTHERN BAPTIST
Theological Seminary

FIRST ANNUAL COMMENCEMENT,

MAY 28, 1860.

PROGRAMME.

MUSIC—*Thanksgiving Anthem.*

PRAYER.

MUSIC — *"Oh, be joyful in the Lord."*

ADDRESS,

BY REV. E. NANLY, D. D. OF ALABAMA.

MUSIC — *"I have set watchmen upon thy walls."*

DIPLOMAS CONFERRED.

HYMN.

1. Soldiers of Christ, in truth arrayed,
   A world in ruins needs your aid;
   A world by sin destroyed and dead;
   A world for which has Saviour bled.

2. Forth to his realms of darkness go,
   Where, like a river's ceaseless flow,
   A tide of souls is drifting down,
   Blasted beneath th' Almighty's frown.

3. Ye heralds shall not power can stay
   That flood upon its gloomy way;
   But God's own law has cleared the plan,
   To save the ruined creature, man.

4. His gospel to the lost proclaim;
   Good news for all, in Jesus' name;
   Let light upon the darkness break,
   That sinners from their death may wake.

5. Morning and evening sow the seed,
   God's grace the effort shall succeed;
   Seed times of tears have oft been found
   With showers of joy and plenty crown'd.

6. We meet to part, but part to meet,
   When earthly labors are complete,
   To join in yet more blest employ,
   In an eternal world of joy.

ADDRESS,

BY REV. J. P. BOYCE, D. D. CHAIRMAN OF THE FACULTY.

MUSIC—*Anthem Doxology.*

BENEDICTION.

GRADUATES.

I. BIBLICAL INTRODUCTION.

E. E. BROWN,	S. C.	WM. G. CASPARI,	VA.
JOHN W. JONES,	VA.		

II. OLD TESTAMENT INTERPRETATION.

ENGLISH DEPARTMENT.

E. E. BROWN,	S. C.	WM. G. CASPARI,	VA.
RUFUS FIGH,	ALA.	E. W. S. NORFIN,	N. C.
T. J. PRICE,	S. C.	CHAS. H. RYLAND,	VA.

ENGLISH AND HEBREW.

J. A. CHAMBLISS,	ALA.	H. K. HATCHER,	VA.
GEO. W. HYDE,	MO.	S. C. B. POWELL,	N. C.
T. R. SHEPHERD,	VA.	CRAWFORD H. TOY,	VA.
		JAS. D. WITT,	VA.

III. NEW TESTAMENT INTERPRETATION.

ENGLISH DEPARTMENT.

W. L. CURRY,	N. C.	W. F. NIGELS,	S. C.
G. W. HYDE,	MO.	S. C. B. POWELL,	N. C.
J. W. JONES,	VA.	T. R. SHEPHERD,	VA.
R. M. MARSH,	N. C.	JAS. D. WITT,	VA.

ENGLISH AND GREEK.

J. A. CHAMBLISS,	ALA.	H. E. HATCHER,	VA.
		CRAWFORD H. TOY,	VA.

IV. SYSTEMATIC THEOLOGY.

ENGLISH DEPARTMENT.

R. B. BOATWRIGHT,	VA.	RUFUS FIGH,	ALA.
JOHN W. JONES,	VA.	WM. G. CASPARI,	VA.

ENGLISH AND LATIN.

CRAWFORD H. TOY,	VA.		

V. POLEMIC THEOLOGY.

W. L. CURRY,	N. C.

VI. HOMILETICS.

J. A. CHAMBLISS,	ALA.	W. L. CURRY,	N. C.
JOHN W. JONES,	VA.	T. R. SHEPHERD,	VA.

VII. ECCLESIASTICAL HISTORY.

WM. G. CASPARI,	VA.	W. L. CURRY,	N. C.
R. M. MARSH,	N. C.	W. F. NIGELS,	S. C.
		CRAWFORD H. TOY,	VA.

VIII. CHURCH GOVERNMENT AND PASTORAL DUTIES.

J. A. CHAMBLISS,	ALA.	W. L. CURRY,	N. C.
H. E. HATCHER,	VA.	G. W. HYDE,	MO.
J. W. JONES,	VA.	CHAS. H. RYLAND,	VA.
T. R. SHEPHERD,	VA.	W. J. SHIPMAN,	VA.
		JAS. D. WITT,	VA.

had compiled a pocket-size edition of classical hymns, which, he told the users of this hymnal, contains "no trash, and no unreal sentiment or unsound doctrine."

It is noteworthy that he included none of his own hymns in *Manly's Choice*. One of them, though, has certainly proven to be a classic, namely, "Soldiers of Christ, in truth arrayed." Manly wrote "Soldiers of Christ, in truth arrayed" for Southern's first annual commencement in 1860, though it appeared in the commencement program without attribution.[65] Manly's hymn has been sung at every graduation since 1860, though not with all of its original stanzas. As Manly penned it, "Soldiers of Christ, in truth arrayed" had six stanzas. From 1871 onwards, though, the original stanzas two and three have been omitted.[66]

"Soldiers of Christ, in truth arrayed"

> Soldiers of Christ, in truth arrayed,
> A world in ruins needs your aid;
> A world by sin destroyed and dead;
> A world for which the Saviour bled.[67]

Baptist circles in this era, see William J. Reynolds, *Companion to Baptist Hymnal* (Nashville: Broadman Press, 1976), 19–20; Paul Harvey, *Redeeming the South: Religious Cultures and Racial Identities among Southern Baptists, 1865–1925* (Chapel Hill: University of North Carolina Press, 1997), 97–100.

65. For proof that it was by Manly, see Platt, "Hymnological Contributions of Basil Manly Jr.," 242 n. 16.

66. Richardson, "Basil Manly, Jr.: Southern Baptist Pioneer in Hymnody," 103–104. Richardson does not provide a reason for the omission of these stanzas. For a possible reason, see below, pages 50–54.

67. The hymn text is cited as it appears in its original form on page 2 of the "Southern Baptist Theological Seminary: First Annual

The first stanza begins with martial imagery that was not uncommon to the classical hymnody of the eighteenth and nineteenth centuries. The most famous of such hymns in Manly's day was Charles Wesley's "Soldiers of Christ, arise" (1749).[68] But Manly was not simply reflecting the classical hymns he deeply loved and appreciated. He was also drawing from biblical passages such as Ephesians 6:10–17 and 2 Timothy 2:4, where the apostle Paul depicts the Christian as a soldier called to engage in spiritual warfare against wicked spiritual powers. For Manly, the Christian (graduate from seminary) is to be a warrior going forth to do battle with the hosts of wickedness and to bring men, women, and children out from the thralldom of such hosts to serve the Lord Jesus. Four years

Commencement, May 28, 1860" (commencement program, 1860, four pages). The exposition of the hymn below follows the enumeration of stanzas as found in the original hymn text and not the numbering according to the post-1871 shortened version. See also the full text of the hymn, with an alteration in spelling ("Savior" instead of "Saviour" in the final line of stanza 1) and some changes in punctuation, in Platt, "Hymnological Contributions of Basil Manly Jr.," 242, and below, pages 151–152.

The four-stanza version of the hymn appears in at least six hymnals published between 1891 and 2008, including *Baptist Hymnal*, ed. William J. Reynolds (Nashville: Convention Press, 1975) hymn 315, in which the final word of stanza 1 was changed from "bled" to "died"; *The Baptist Hymnal*, ed. Wesley L. Forbis (Nashville: Convention Press, 1991) hymn 574, in which the final word of stanza 1 has been changed back to "bled"; *Baptist Hymnal*, ed. Mike Harland (Nashville: LifeWay, 2008) hymn 661. The author is indebted for the information in this paragraph to David L. Gregory (e-mail message to Michael A. G. Haykin, December 19, 2008).

68. Manly included this hymn in all three of his hymnals. See Platt, "Hymnological Contributions of Basil Manly Jr.," 180, 206, 221.

before Manly wrote this hymn, he had told the graduating class of the University of North Carolina:

> I have no sad words of farewell, no sighs of trembling anticipation to breathe into your ears. Rather would I sound the cheering trumpet call, rather hail you as fellow soldiers marching to the battle, rather join my voice with the voices that come from numberless posts of honor and of duty, claiming the consecration of fervent piety, the active energies of young hearts. I will not say *Farewell*—and bid you go forth into the world—but *Welcome*, as you press out into life. Welcome to the field of conflict, welcome to the certain triumph, welcome to the armies of truth and holiness.[69]

Over thirty years later, Manly made similar remarks in a graduation address that he gave at Newton Theological Institution in the year before his death: the "trophies" of the faithful minister's "success are not in battles won by bloodshed," but "in souls won from sin, in lives lifted and purified, in sorrows lightened and doubts dispelled, in victims rescued from ruin, in saints fitted for heaven, in glory brought to Jesus."[70]

_____

69. Basil Manly, Jr., *A Sermon, Preached by Appointment of the Senior Class of the University of North Carolina, June 2, 1856* (Richmond: H. K. Ellyson, 1856), 16.

70. "Free Research and Firm Faith," *Christian Index* (October 15, 1891), 2–3. See also the use of martial imagery in Manly's *Halting on This Side of Jordan, or, Shall Your Brethren Go to War, and Shall Ye Sit Here?* (Greenville, S.C., tract, eight pages). An electronic edition of this tract prepared by the University of North Carolina at Chapel Hill is available in *Documenting the American South* (http://docsouth.unc.edu/imls/manlyb/

Empowering Christians in their warfare, as Gregory
A. Wills has noted, is the "truth," or the body of Christian
doctrine.[71] It is only as Christians are "arrayed" in or submissive to this truth that they can be of help to anyone in
the world. As has been noted above, Manly believed that
this truth was found supremely in the Bible, which, as he
put it in the late 1880s, is "truly the Word of God, having both infallible truth and divine authority in all that it
affirms or enjoins."[72]

The next two lines of this first stanza paint a deeply
pessimistic, though utterly realistic, view of the world
of humanity. It is "in ruins." It is "destroyed and dead."[73]
And the culprit is "sin." Some of Manly's other hymns also
seek to express graphically the devastation caused by sin.
Ruined by sin, human beings are "weak and wounded,
sick and sore."[74] Owing to the ravages of sin, the human
heart is "vile," the "mind depraved," and the will rebel-
lious, so that in the sight of God the totality of human life
is "polluted." Men and women are thus in need of deliv-

---

manlyb.html; accessed January 3, 2009). For a selection from this tract,
see below, pages 209–213.

    71. Wills, "Manly, Basil, Jr.," 418.

    72. Basil Manly, Jr., *Bible Doctrine of Inspiration*, 90.

    73. In another context, Manly can speak of the world as "perish-
ing" (*A Call to the Ministry* [Greenville, S.C.: G. E. Elford's Job Press,
1866], 16).

    74. "Come all who feel your sins a load," stanza 4. The text of this
hymn can be found below, pages 179–180. This line is taken directly
from Joseph Hart's (1712–1768) "Come, ye sinners, poor and wretched,"
stanza 1, a hymn that Manly included in all three of his hymnals (Platt,
"Hymnological Contributions of Basil Manly Jr.," 162, 201, 218).

erance from both "the guilt and power of sin."[75] In fact, so deeply embedded and pervasive is sin that Manly can confess, "No terrors have my soul deterred / Nor good-ness wooed me from my sin" and what he, and all other human sinners "deserve" is God's "deepest wrath."[76] In the systematic expression of Manly's Abstract of Principles, human beings are born with a "nature corrupt and wholly opposed to God and His law, are under condemnation, and as soon as they are capable of moral action, become actual transgressors."[77]

In contrast to such sinfulness, God is a "God of spot-less purity." And the question naturally presents itself: "How shall sinners worship" God or even draw near to Him?[78] The answer is sketched in the fourth line of this stanza: despite its conscious, unmitigated rebellion against God, this world is yet "a world for which the Sav-ior bled." Though committed to particular redemption, as has been noted above, Manly has no problem speaking of Christ's dying for the world, for this is the way Scripture sometimes speaks.[79] In one hymn in particular, "Come all

75. "Lord, I deserve thy deepest wrath," stanzas 2 and 4. This hymn can be found in Platt, "Hymnological Contributions of Basil Manly Jr.," 238–239 and in this volume, pages 135–136.

76. "Lord, I deserve thy deepest wrath," stanza 1.

As Manly noted on another occasion, "The idea that God is too good to punish the evil doer is the half-way house to infidelity" (cited in Mueller, *History of Southern Baptist Theological Seminary*, 86).

77. Abstract of Principles VI.

78. "Holy, holy, holy Lord," stanza 4. This hymn can be found in Platt, "Hymnological Contributions of Basil Manly Jr.," 237 and in this volume, page 134.

79. See, for instance, 1 John 2:2.

who feel your sins a load," written in 1871, Manly spells out how Christ's death decisively resolves the sin issue. Manly urges all who "feel your sins a load" to come and view Christ:

> A meek and lowly Saviour see,
> His love is vast, His grace is free;
> To Him your guilt and burden take....
>
> Wounded for love of us was He,
> And bruised for our iniquity,
> To heal our souls, behold Him bleed![80]

The main biblical passage from which Manly is drawing his thought here is, of course, Isaiah 53, long used as a key text by those upholding the teaching that Christ, the sinless one, suffered in the stead of sinners.

The omitted stanzas

> Forth to the realms of darkness go,
> Where, like a river's ceaseless flow,
> A tide of souls is drifting down,
> Blasted beneath th' Almighty's frown.
>
> No human skill nor power can stay
> That flood upon its gloomy way;
> But God's own love devised the plan
> To save the ruined creature, man.

---

80. "Come all who feel your sins a load," stanzas 1–3. This hymn can be found in Platt, "Hymnological Contributions of Basil Manly Jr.," 240 and in this volume, pages 179–180.

As noted above, these stanzas have not been generally sung since 1871. That was the year Manly left Southern to become the president of Georgetown College.[81] It seems unlikely the stanzas were dropped without Manly's agreement, for when he rejoined the faculty in 1879, the omitted stanzas were not reinserted, suggesting that Manly ultimately approved of the change. As a compiler of hymns who had made the occasional change to the hymns in his hymnals, he would have known that hymns, unlike poems, can undergo minor changes if this enables them to be better used by congregations. A clue as to why these stanzas may have been omitted must wait, however, until stanzas 4 and 5 are examined.

The battlefields on which the soldiers of Christ have been called to fight (stanza 1) are here depicted in the second and third stanzas as "realms of darkness" filled with "souls" who are heading for destruction. Using the imagery of a river that is in spate and whose waters cannot be held back by any human agency, Manly is able to depict powerfully the utter hopelessness of the human condition. Sinful men and women, unreconciled to a holy God and thus under His wrath, are moment by moment being swept along by the stream of history to the final judgment of God.[82]

---

81. As noted by David L. Gregory (e-mail message to Michael A. G. Haykin, December 19, 2008).

82. For Manly's thinking about this final judgment, see Abstract of Principles XX. "Serious views...of life and of death, of judgment and eternity" were, in Manly's estimation, "indispensable to real religion" (*A Sermon, Preached by Appointment of the Senior Class*, 7).

Recitation Hall at Georgetown College, where Manly, Jr.
taught classes on biblical interpretation and Hebrew

(Photo Source: Georgetown College
Belle of the Blue Yearbook—1898)

But there is hope, for though human ingenuity and energy cannot save "the ruined creature, man," God certainly can.[83] His love wrought a plan of salvation whereby, as was declared in the first stanza, Christ bled and died for the sinful world. Henceforth, those who have come to embrace that plan of salvation are constrained to cry out, as Manly puts it in another hymn, "To Thy grace all hope we owe."[84]

"Let light…break"

> His gospel to the lost proclaim;
> Good news for all in Jesus' name;
> Let light upon the darkness break,
> That sinners from their death may wake.
>
> Morning and evening sow the seed;
> God's grace the effort shall succeed;
> Seed-times of tears have oft been found
> With sheaves of joy and plenty crown'd.

Near the close of his 1856 address to the graduating class of the University of North Carolina, in which Manly spent much of his time reflecting on the vital importance and impact of the Scriptures, he noted that wherever, at the time of the Reformation, the "Bible was brought out of the cloisters and given to men…there was light." But

---

83. In the final stanza of "Jesus, my Lord, I own thee God" (for the hymn, see below, page 135), Manly similarly states, "Thou, gracious Lord, my soul would own, / The power to save is thine alone."

84. "Holy, holy, holy Lord," stanza 4.

"where it was absent, darkness reigned."[85] Here, in stanzas 4 and 5 of the seminary hymn, Manly can use the same imagery with respect to the preaching of the gospel: wherever the gospel, "good news…in Jesus' name," is proclaimed, there is light in the midst of "darkness."

Note that if the second and third stanzas, discussed above, are retained, then the possessive pronoun in the phrase "His gospel" must refer back to the subject of the last two lines of stanza 3, namely God the Father. Stanza 3 ends by extolling His love that devised the plan of salvation, and hence it is His gospel that was to be proclaimed to "the lost." With the omission of stanzas 2 and 3, as occurred from 1871 onwards, the possessive pronoun of "His gospel" now refers back to the subject of the final line of stanza 1—namely, Jesus. Dropping stanzas 2 and 3 may then be understood to have been done for stylistic reasons, to make the connection closer between stanza 1, which finishes with Jesus' bleeding for the world, and stanza 4, which opens with the gospel of His saving blood being proclaimed to a lost world. In this way, the entire hymn becomes tightly Christocentric.

The use of the imperative "let" in the third line of stanza 4—"Let light upon the darkness break"—recalls similar terminology in the Genesis account of creation: "Let there be light," for example, in Genesis 1:3.[86] And just as the divine fiat in Genesis 1 brings to pass all that it is designed to accomplish, so too with the proclama-

---

85. Basil Manly, Jr., *A Sermon, Preached by Appointment of the Senior Class*, 15–16.

86. See the similar wording in Genesis 1:6, 9, 11, 14, 15, 20, 24.

tion of the luminiferous gospel. But not only is divine power active in the gospel proclamation; Christ's soldiers (stanza 1) must also be active in seeking to win the lost. They are to go forth "to the realms of darkness" (stanza 2), or, as Manly puts it in another hymn, "Let the light shine,…/The blessed news to all men take."[87] These two aspects of evangelism, the sovereignty of God's grace and the activity of human proclamation to all and sundry, are well captured in stanza 5 with Manly's skillful use of Psalm 126:5–6.[88]

The need of the church, and her ministers, to be passionate about evangelism and missions was a constant refrain in Manly's thinking. "Any church that ceases to be evangelistic," Manly was convinced, "will soon cease to be evangelical."[89] And in one of his most powerful published addresses, *A Call to the Ministry*, which he gave at the seminary in the year following the Civil War, Manly declared:

> Now we need numbers in the Ministry. The plenteous, perishing harvest wails out a despairing cry for more laborers. But we need purity more than numbers; we need intelligence more than numbers; we

---

87. "There is a light which shines from heaven," stanza 5. This hymn can be found in Platt, "Hymnological Contributions of Basil Manly Jr.," 239–240.

88. "They that sow in tears shall reap in joy. He that goeth forth and weepeth, bearing precious seed, shall doubtless come again with rejoicing, bringing his sheaves with him" (KJV). See the similar use of this Psalm in Manly's 1886 hymn "Work, for the day is coming," stanza 2 (Platt, "Hymnological Contributions of Basil Manly Jr.," 241).

89. "A Sketch of the History of the Evidences of Christianity," *Seminary Magazine*, 3 (March 1890): 90.

need zeal more than numbers. Above all, we need consecrated men, men who have stood beneath the Cross, till their very souls are dyed with Jesus' blood, and a love like His for perishing millions has been kindled within them. We long for such men, but for such only, as are willing to endure hardness as good soldiers of Jesus Christ.[90]

"Yet more blest employ"

> We meet to part, but part to meet,
> When earthly labors are complete,
> To join in yet more blest employ,
> In an eternal world of joy.

The evangelistic activism pervading the other stanzas is found here as well in this poignant final stanza.[91] Christian meetings, like the many commencements at which this hymn has been sung, are designed to send people out into ministry: "we meet to part." But as Manly envisioned it, such ministry and gospel labor had a goal, "an eternal world of joy" where all Christians will meet, never to part again. Manly's hymn thus points the singer to eternity.[92] And as such, the hymn reflects the common perspective of nineteenth-century evangelicalism that life is to be lived

---

90. *Call to the Ministry*, 12. For this address, see below, pages 173–178.

91. On the poignancy of this final stanza, see R. Albert Mohler, Jr., "For the Glory of God," *Southern Seminary Magazine*, 71, no. 2 (Summer 2003): i.

92. Mohler, Jr., "For the Glory of God," i.

BASIL MANLY
BORN AT EDGEFIELD DIST., S.C.,
DEC. 19, 1825,
DIED AT LOUISVILLE KY.,
JAN. 31, 1892.
HE SERVED HIS OWN GENERATION
BY THE WILL OF GOD.

MANLY
PASTOR IN SUMTER COUNTY, ALA.,
AND OF FIRST BAPTIST CHURCH, RICHMOND, VA.
FOUNDER AND PRESIDENT,
RICHMOND FEMALE INSTITUTE.
ONE OF THE FOUNDERS AND FIRST PROFESSORS
OF SOUTHERN BAPTIST THEOLOGICAL
SEMINARY, 1859-71, AND 1879-92.
PRESIDENT GEORGETOWN COLLEGE KY., 1871-9.

sub specie aeternitatis, and it is this orientation that helps establish what it means to be a Christian.

What, though, is the "yet more blest employ" in that "eternal world" of which this final stanza speaks? One possible answer can be found in a hymn that Manly wrote nearly a quarter of a century later in 1884, "Work, for the day is coming."[93] In the second stanza of this hymn we find Manly using Psalm 126 in a way that was reminiscent of "Soldiers of Christ, in truth arrayed":

> What we now sow in sadness,
> Then we shall reap in joy;
> Hope will be changed to gladness,
> Praise be our best employ.[94]

Is the "blest employ" of "Soldiers of Christ, in truth arrayed" the same as the "best employ" of "Work, for the day is coming"— namely, praise and worship? Quite possibly, for in 1856, four years before Manly wrote the seminary hymn, he had confidently stated that the highest goal of human existence is living for "the glory of God." Compared to "the grandeur of this lofty aim, all others become insignificant. In the radiance from this luminous pinnacle, all other lights are comprehended and lost."[95]

---

93. For the historical context of this hymn, see Richardson, "Basil Manly, Jr.: Southern Baptist Pioneer in Hymnody," 106.

94. "Work, for the day is coming," stanza 2.

95. Basil Manly, Jr., *A Sermon, Preached by Appointment of the Senior Class*, 12.

SELECTIONS FROM
Basil Manly, Sr.

Basil Manly, Sr.

1

On the emancipation of slaves[1]

Slavery is an evil under which this country has long groaned. Introduced at first from motives of avarice, it has been perpetuated in this country partly as a convenience, partly through necessity, without exciting...any general apprehension. But now its prevalence and continual increase are such as compels us seriously to ask, whether there be not danger in its further continuance; while the injuries inflicted on its wretched victims make the long neglected appeal to the feelings of humanity to devise, if possible, a plan for its removal. On a question of such extent and importance, and so little subjected to experiment at the present, it will be difficult to decide

---

1. Basil Manly, Sr., "On the Emancipation of Slaves," April, 1821, Manly Family Papers, South Carolina Baptist Historical Collection, James Buchanan Duke Library, Furman University, Greenville, S.C. Delivered in the wake of the political crisis that led to the Missouri Compromise, this college speech can be interpreted in different ways. At a time when many Southerners still supported the American Colonization Society, Manly might have believed in emancipation, might have been taking a side for the sake of debate, or could actually have been defending slavery in it. For more on this speech and its interpretation, see Fuller, *Chaplain to the Confederacy*, 32–35.

much with certainty; but as truth is to be elicited only in the freedom of discussion, he who may argue even on the wrong side of the question will not have been occupied in vain. But whatever obscurity may rest on some parts of this question, a few considerations will sufficiently show the danger to which slavery subjects us, and demonstrate the necessity of an immediate provision against it.

Inveterate and opposite prejudices are entertained on this subject by the inhabitants of different sections of our country. While, however, these prejudices were confined to the fire-sides of the citizens, the states of the union lived together in confederate amity.... But now the case is different. These prejudices have been introduced into the national councils; and the period seems fast approaching, when...the people of the country as a nation must come to a fixed and final determination. A collision of interests and feelings has already been produced on a question that is but the preliminary, if not the certain precursor of the final question on the subject of slavery; and...no doubt can be entertained but they will again call up a contention characterized by the intensity and rashness of party feeling which shall deeply agitate the whole continent. The parties are already formed; and, while the ground of difference remains, which is neither more nor less than slavery, opinions and feelings so discordant...cannot easily be reconciled. The one party will ever be the revilers of the other.... If, therefore, we waive the final determination of this question, under the vain hope that the future will find us as peaceful and united as the past has done—we allow prejudices to remain, jealousness to ferment, parties to become more distinct and decided. And is any friend of his country prepared for the event, when, threatened by an envious and powerful foe from without, some subject, such as that which lately distracted the councils of our national assembly, shall again call up a party dispute? I confess that…I am not prepared for the event, but am one of those who think that the point in dispute should be amicably settled as speedily as possible and that if contending parties are not reconciled, the fair fabric of our union (I shudder to think of it) must totter to its basis.

This argument for emancipation, drawn from necessity, is in itself of weight, but it is strengthened by other consideration.

Slavery seems to be utterly repugnant to the spirit of our republican institutions. While the framers of our constitution recognized most distinctly the principle that all men are naturally free and equal, with the very hand that subscribed to it, and fought to maintain it, they held the chain that bound a portion of their fellow men to perpetual servitude. The stigma which attaches to hypocrisy and tyranny is indeed wiped away in this instance by the reflection that to them slavery was unavoidable. But the inconsistency between slavery and a perfect equality and freedom can never be removed so long as those terms embrace the same ideas they do at present. And who can say that when the memory of '76 shall have faded from the breast of the young American, and the voice of a Washington, after the lapse of years, shall have vibrated feebly through the continent involved in luxury, and wrapt in a careless security, who can say that some rich and powerful combination will not trample on the liberties and privileges of the common people, whom many are even now learning to consider as little superior to their slaves?

The slave population, increasing so much faster than that of the whites, will ultimately be dangerous to the lives and liberties of the people of this country.... Suppose them then...to have learned the story of our revolutionary struggle, and to have caught an inspiring glance from Liberty which gladdens every American heart, and lights up every American habitation but their own; and...suppose them to be able to number a population equal to that of whites, and then tell me if the conviction is not irresistible that they will be prepared for any act of violence to which a long oppression can prompt a revengeful mind. They will be *prepared*.... But if to the evils of slavery you add the horrors of despair...the horrors of St. Domingo[2] will be light in comparison to those which his fury will meditate.

So far we have argued on the plea of self preservation which, being the first law of our nature, acknowledges no contrary rule of action.... If the emancipation and transportation of slaves be necessary to the permanent safety and interest of our country, we should be justified in sending them, though but to relapse into the native ferocity and cheerless ignorance of the African character; we should be culpable in not doing it even at the hazard of more than their value. Emancipation can at least be defended on this

---

2. Here Manly refers to the only successful slave rebellion in the history of the Western Hemisphere: that in Haiti, where years of violent unrest resulted in the creation of an independent black republic.

principle (self-preservation). But justice demands it at our hands for that ill-fated people. And their injuries and long servitude call upon us loudly to return them "their own with usury," not only to restore to them the enjoyment of their ancient rights and privileges, but, along with these, to endeavor according to our ability to bestow on them the blessings of civil and religious society. This demand of justice is not evaded by laying the fault of their captivity on those who first introduced them among us. The fault of our ancestors, or of the universe, cannot disavow the law of Heaven which brings all men into this world equally free. And however the laws of inheritance sanctioned by the constitution of the country, and the impossibility of effecting their emancipation at once, may palliate the charge of tyranny and injustice to which we are exposed; they can never wholly vindicate us from it; nor can they for a moment free us from the obligation of attempting to serve the cause of freedom in every practicable method.

But what is a practicable method — one which promises to serve the double purpose of our safety and their freedom?... [A] little reflection will show that no plan can be readily devised, except colonization, which has a reasonable prospect of success. To emancipate and drive them from state to state as wretched outcasts from the protection of civil government, will be more cruel than the most abject servitude. To invest them with the privileges of freedom in promiscuous distribution amongst us, or to assign them a territory even in the remotest of our western wilds, would be fatal either to them or ourselves. So that question of emancipation at length resolves itself into that of colonization at a distance from us. If this be not politic and right, that is not. The faint glimmerings of hope which cheered the gloom of slavery are then shut out forever; and the only duty of the master is to alleviate its necessary evils by executing as far as possible the blessed laws of justice and mercy.

But colonization has not yet been demonstrated to be impolitic and wrong. The objection against it can be met with arguments of equal validity.... I appeal to the golden rule of our Savior, which no human authority can in any case weaken...and I ask any serious, impartial man what would be his choice under circumstances of slavery? Would it not be to encounter worse than the alleged difficulties [of colonization] if they should be the price of his freedom?...

The difficulty and expense of the colonization system are indeed matters of serious moment. It is not however expected that the plan can be carried into complete and full operation at once. It must be the work of time. The period has not yet arrived when a direct and extensive interference on the part of government would be prudent. All that can now be asked of government is just to admit the principle, to encourage the formation of benevolent societies which have in view this grand object, and to protect with their flag these sons of misfortune as they are returning to their long lost home. When the principle of colonization is once admitted, the work will of itself go on. A cause of so much benevolence and justice will rarely fail to command the energies of the good. And I cannot avoid indulging the pleasing anticipation, that in the progress of civilization, of liberty and religion which are all engaged to support this cause, the time may yet arrive when this government may with propriety declare herself the friend of universal emancipation; when all America shall lift an united voice over the abodes of slavery and wretchedness, and proclaim an eternal jubilee.

2

Promoting revival

Edgefield, July 29, 1822[1]

Dear brother,

It is with pleasure I am now able to tell you of the good things which God is doing for us at Stephen's Creek.... The meeting began on Friday, and nothing special appeared until near the close of the exercises on Saturday, when suddenly, and like an electric shock, the Divine power seemed to be poured out on the whole congregation. As many as 25 or 30 rose with an involuntary effort, and without particular invitation, came up crying for mercy, and begging the people of God to pray for them. It was truly astonishing—I never saw such things before—so universal an effect; such deep and agonizing sorrow, attended with so little noise and confusion.

...On Sunday the effect was still greater. Although we had been longing and looking for a revival...yet after the first transport of joy and gratitude had subsided, I

---

1. Basil Manly, Sr., "Revival at Edgefield," *Southern Intelligencer* 1 (August 10, 1822): 127. The church at Little Stephen's Creek (or Little Stevens' Creek) was one of several congregations Manly served as pastor in rural Edgefield, South Carolina.

had most distressing doubts and fears. My heart was cold
and callous, and even indifferent in prayer. I was in a distressing state of inquiry as to the cause of these feelings:
whether God was showing me that it was not his work,
and that it would soon subside; or whether I was to learn
that it was not our prayers nor preaching, but his gracious arm alone, that we might be deeply humbled before
him. [Another brother] and myself being mutually under
these views and feelings, set out the next week following through the neighborhood, to see what God the Lord
would say to us. The further we went the more were our
hearts strengthened and I bless God for the great things
we saw and felt on that day. The hand of the Lord is in the
work, and in a most powerful manner. In one settlement
not far from the meeting-house, the people have literally
left off their domestic business, and are going night and
day, far and near, where they can hear of a prayer meeting.
As the fruit of this revival, which is fast increasing and
seems like to spread, I have baptized twenty-five within
the last three weeks; sixteen of them last Friday at Stephen's Creek, when more than a thousand persons were
present; and two in the village of Edgefield yesterday.

Truly yours,
B. Manly

Edgefield, August 29, 1822[2]

My dear sir,

Having just returned to my residence to seek a little needful repose from a long train of varied engagements in the service of our common Lord, I…find in your paper… from a letter of mine…a short account of the revival of religion in Edgefield. That letter was hastily written in a short interval of extreme weariness, and…necessarily embraced but an imperfect view of the rise and progress of so glorious a work among us. Believing it to be not only interesting, but often attended with results the most important, to mark…the whole course of the Divine mercy in Revivals of Religion, and to publish it among the friends of Zion, I take the liberty…to make the following statement.

…Some of the brethren seemed much engaged in prayer for a revival of God's work among them, and…were "hoping against hope," …to see "the times of refreshing come from the presence of the Lord."[3] On the Friday before the second Sabbath in May, which had been appointed by the Edgefield Baptist Association as a day of fasting, humiliation and prayer, the church assembled. A larger congregation than usual, both of the whites and blacks, who on that day were liberated from work by their owners for the purpose, attended with us…. On the Sabbath morning following, which was our regular monthly meeting, one person, a lady, was baptized…. At our monthly

2. Basil Manly, Sr., "Revival in Edgefield," *Southern Intelligencer* 1 (September 7, 1822): 142–143.

3. Acts 3:19.

meeting in June, the tokens of the Revival became visible among the brethren. At that time, in church conference,... we conversed freely on what had been our feelings and prevailing desires in relation to this subject since the last meeting. And while we talked, "our hearts burned within us."[4] The trickling tear from eyes that had long looked for the coming of God, marked the first signal of His approach. And before the meeting closed...it was proposed from the chair, that...those who felt disposed should *publicly agree to pray for a Revival.* Many of the brethren and sisters solemnly covenanted together...that they would habitually be found in mutual prayer to God, that he would revive his work, in their own hearts, and generally among his people. Here were the travailings of Zion. The place was made sweet and awful by the presence of the Lord. And many retired pensively away, greatly wondering at the things which should come to pass. We also...mutually agreed that in the interval of our meetings we would exhort and encourage our fellow members to attend more assiduously to their church and prayer meetings, and be otherwise diligently and faithfully engaged in duty.

[O]n the fifth Sabbath of June and day before it,... [a long-planned union] meeting now came on.... [On] Saturday evening, just at the close of the meeting..., and while the exercises were proceeding calmly, there was a sudden and powerful *moving* among the congregation, as if by the force of electricity. Our first feelings were those of mute astonishment; and even the minister who was up

---

4. Luke 24:32.

at the time, scarcely knew what to think of it. But soon the mighty power of God was manifested by numbers of keenly convicted souls rushing up to the stand, with deep agitation and trembling, begging the prayers of God's people.

It was truly a "shaking among the dry bones."[5] On the next day the effect seemed to be much increased. And from the number of gracious experiences which have since dated the first impression at this meeting, we believe it was indeed "one of the days of the Son of Man."[6] The drooping head of Zion began now to be raised. Our hopes revived; and the issue has exceeded our highest expectations. Since the 2nd Sabbath of July, I have baptized on credible profession of a living faith in the dear Redeemer, fifty-eight persons. On tomorrow eleven more are to receive the ordinance, who have already been admitted as candidates for it; and probably many more, who are believed to have recently "passed from death unto life."[7] The Lord is convicting and converting souls on the right hand and on the left; and daily reports meet our joyful ears of the triumphs of redeeming grace. The work seems still to be deepening and spreading. The young and middle-aged are almost exclusively the subjects of it.

No noise, no disorder attends it; nor is the voice of the preacher even interrupted, but by the broken and half stifled sobs, and heart-felt sighs of the mourning penitents. It is impossible for us now to doubt of its being the work of God. And we indulge a strong hope that our dark and

---

5. See Ezekiel 37:7.
6. Luke 17:22.
7. 1 John 3:14.

barren land is about once more to be visited with extensive and copious showers of divine love. Rejoice with us,
my brothers, and help us to praise that God Lord Jesus,
who has done such great things for us. And oh! Let all
the dear lovers of the slain Lamb be deeply humbled and
mutually united with one heart and one soul to pray for a
general revival among us.[8]

...With sentiments of respect, I am, dear sir, yours,
etc.,   — B. Manly

---

8. The Edgefield Revival spread across the state of South Carolina
and spilled over into Georgia. Manly preached widely in both states
and won a reputation as an evangelist. His work in Edgefield built up
three congregations and he personally baptized hundreds of new converts during the revival. For more on the Edgefield Revival, see Fuller,
Chaplain to the Confederacy, 43–55.

3

Dealing with the death of children

Diary entry, July 15, 1829[1]

> On Wednesday evening, July 15, 1829, 12 o'clock
> at night, precisely, our youngest child [Zebulon
> Rudulph Manly] died. He had been taken ill of a
> dysentery, on the Sabbath morning previously, and
> after a short period of extreme suffering, breathed
> his last. Had he lived 30 hours longer he would have
> been two years old. My Dear little Rudulph, thou art
> gone from me to the arms of thy Father above.

Diary entry, July 16, 1829[2]

> At six o'clock, [a fellow Baptist minister] performed
> the funeral service at our dwelling, for our dear, little
> departed Babe…. A very large assembly were pres-
> ent. I went to the grave accompanied by…my little

1. Basil Manly, Sr., Church Journal, Manly Family Papers, Southern Baptist Historical Collection, James Buchanan Duke Library,
Furman University, Greenville, S.C
2. Basil Manly, Sr., Church Journal.

Basil. The child though only three years and a half old, seemed to know what it all meant and asked many questions concerning his brother throughout the day.

About an hour after the death of Rudulph, Basil, who was sleeping in a crib, waked [*sic*] up and looked for his brother. Not finding him where he was used to lie, he asked for him, and being told that he was dead, he burst into a flood of tears, and said that he had no brother now. He would not be pacified until I had showed him the corpse. The features were all so natural and sweet, that he seemed to think him only sleeping and was quiet for the night. In the morning, however, he continued at intervals to ask for his brother and to make some remark about him which, proceeding from him, was truly affecting. He was going about the house and crying most of the day, speaking of his brother and death, until the company began to assemble for the funeral, which attracted his attention. At the grave, he eyed the coffin with undivided attention and when it was let down into the grave he stepped to the brink holding my hand, and continued to look earnestly until the grave was entirely filled. My only desire concerning him is that he may be God's child.

And in the affliction we have felt, it is our desire to bless him that takes as well as him that gives. I think I see already much wisdom and goodness in this stroke.

Diary entry, November 6, 1830 [3]

Death of my child. November 6, 1830, Saturday. This evening at a quarter past six my dear little John Waldo died. His disease seemed to lie in his chest and he obtained no relief from the moment he was taken. I was absent at the [Charleston Baptist] Association, but the Lord took care of my wife and strengthened her to close the eyes of the dear child with a quiet resignation. When the business of the Association ended, I took a horse and rode on ahead of my company, and learned…35 miles from town that my Babe was dead. "I was dumb, I opened not my mouth, because thou didst it."[4] In response to this and a similar bereavement last year, I trust I can say with Jacob, "If I be bereaved of my children, I am bereaved."[5] The child had attained, within a day and a half, seven months of age and was one of the most interesting Babes I ever saw. But the will of the Lord is done and I have not a word to say in opposition to it.

---

3. Basil Manly, Sr., "Diary I (1826–1833)," p. 148 (November 6, 1830), Manly Family Papers, William Stanley Hoole Special Collections Library, University of Alabama, Tuscaloosa.

4. Psalm 39:9.

5. Genesis 43:14.

4

On the death of children[1]

Reflection on the *uncertainty of human prospects*, and the *brevity of life* should chasten our worldly attachments.

As pilgrims we are reminded that this is not our rest, and are forbidden to love the world or the things of it....

With regard to children, particularly, as so large a portion of their lives is spent in helplessness, and so much of their future well-being depends on the care which is bestowed on their infancy and youth, God has opened *two abundant* fountains in nature to supply the streams of affection.

They are a part of our selves. They take our names, wear our features, and our blood runs in their veins....

The care and attention bestowed on their helpless years endear and strengthen affection — and for the same reason that benevolence is a stronger affection than grati-

1. Basil Manly, Sr., "Bereavement of Children," sermon preached on November 14, 1830, Basil Manly Manuscripts Sermons and Notes, James P. Boyce Centennial Library Archives, Southern Baptist Theological Seminary, Louisville, Ky. Manly based this sermon for John Waldo Manly (see above, page 77), on Genesis 43:14, "If I be bereaved of my children, I am bereaved."

tude…the love of a parent to a child is greater than that of a child to a parent.

Bereavement of children therefore is on this account more poignant and at the same time, the disparity of grief is further increased by the fact that parents have fewer mitigations than children for the most part have.

As to the death of parents, the course of nature leads us to anticipate their departure and the expectation diminishes the shock of this final fall.

But that of children is unexpected. We did not think to survive them, had hoped to be proffered in declining years to live again [with] them, and thus to mingle…with future generations.

Add to this, that in almost every instance there is some peculiarly touching circumstance which is affecting to a parent's mind, more than to that of any other relation….

We are not surprised therefore at the feelings which some have manifested — David for Absalom; Jacob for Joseph — It is what many feel.

This however was immoderate — Jacob afterwards was brought to a better mind. Under more complicated evils of the same kind he said, "If I be bereaved, etc."

Let it be so — explained by Esther 4:16; Acts 21:14.

How shall we hope to arrive at such a state of mind?

Passing by those considerations which are a common relief to all the afflicted, we shall notice those which seem to have contributed to Jacob's resignation.

1. A perception of the hand of God as our Father in it. In the supposed of loss of Joseph, the peculiar circumstances

turned his mind more to the immediate causes. Now he sees the hand of God. Wise, good, merciful, all-sufficient, etc. "I was dumb, etc."

2. The subduing affect of repeated affliction. At first he was like a bullock unaccustomed. What could have persuaded him when he said, "My son shall not go," that he could be brought to consent? The Lord knows how to make us bow to receive the yoke.

3. The conviction that in dismissing Benjamin he was acting out of a sense of duty, as pointed out by Providence. It would seem Jacob had a view to the welfare of them all and probably might not have been without some expectation that the promise to Abraham was now to be fulfilled. Genesis 15:13–14. It is true to some as Joseph said, God sends our children before to save life…. They go before to people the new celestial country, and wait to welcome us to our final home.

 Let us cease to weep.
 1. Moderate attachment — make not food for grief.
 2. As Joseph said to Rachel, God with more propriety
  may say to us, "Am not I better than 10 sons?"

[*Marginal note:*] Preached on Sabbath after the death of my dear little John, who died November 6, 1830 at ¼ past 6 of Saturday evening. I was absent at the time. This was preached Sabbath, November 14, 1830.

[*Marginal note:*] To this sermon Mrs. Ker Boyce (mother of Dr. J. P. Boyce) referred her conversion. (Sarah Manly)

Modern photograph of First Baptist Church
of Charleston, South Carolina

5

Lydia Frierson[1]

Monday, June 22, 1829

I have received two visits from a coloured woman lately (Lydia Frierson) who in the honesty of her heart confesses to me that her master compels her to live in constant adultery with him. The woman is a member of the church, and seems broken hearted on account of it. Although this was secret known only to God and herself she has abstained from Communion for years on account of it. I advised her to remonstrate kindly with her master; and firmly and decidedly to tell him that she could not consent to sin if he would not hear her mild remonstrance. She has been to me today to say that she has used every means in her power, and that he threatens her most dreadfully if she resists him. I assured her that it is better for her to die, than to sin, that she surely can prevent the evil if she be resolute and firm, and that

1. Basil Manly, Sr., Church Journal, Manly Family Papers, South Carolina Baptist Historical Collection, James Buchanan Duke Library, Furman University, Greenville, S.C.

God will not hold her guiltless while any possible means of preventing it, even to the risk of life itself, remains untried. I have told her that I will not mention the matter to the church for a season, waiting to see how the case will terminate. Poor Creature! I believe her to be sincere and she now seems wasted and broken hearted on the account.

December, 1833

I purchased this same woman [from]…one of the heirs of Mr. Frierson and she is now our worthy and respected old nurse.

6

Some thoughts on sacred music[1]

…Sacred music is clearly on the best authorities a part of the worship of God, and a means of grace…. He that made man knew what was in him, and what would affect him and has exhorted his children in the Scriptures to "teach and admonish both sons and one another, in Psalms, and Hymns, and spiritual songs, singing and making melody in their hearts unto the Lord." See Ephesians 5:19; Colossians 3:16.

In the Christian church its use is in part *Instruction*, "Teaching one another, etc." It is not to be a performance of sounds or syllables, but of *words*, in musical tone, which …are suited to edify the mind and establish it in the truths of the Gospel. The reason for the accompaniment of musical sounds is that the effect of these in softening the feelings and increasing the susceptibility of the soul may prepare the way and assist the effect of divine truth….

1. Basil Manly, Sr., "Some Thoughts on Sacred Music, Delivered in Substance at the anniversary of a Society in the Baptist Church, for the Cultivation of Sacred Music, Charleston, South Carolina, June 27, 1832," Manly Family Papers, William Stanley Hoole Special Collections Library, University of Alabama, Tuscaloosa.

Another part of its design is *admonition* and *encouragement*. This it does as well by the exhilarating, animating or rousing effect of sounds upon the feelings, as by the stimulating nature of the truths conveyed…. In short, music is a *style of language* which seeks to affect the passions, but so as to turn them into a religious channel….

[Then] a very principal design of psalmody is *Praise, we therein praise God.*

It might be expected that on this occasion I should say something on the admissibility of instrumental music in the worship of the Christian church….[2] The subject… has been viewed as a question of *conscience* and as a question of *expediency*. Considering it in the latter view, some have thought that the expense of providing instruments… might well be spared, and the same amounts of money regularly devoted to the spread of the Gospel in some other way might be expected to do far more good…. It may be sufficient to remark that the question of expediency in relation to congregational expenses may be determined by the same rules which should regulate a conscientious individual in ordering his own style of living. If a private Christian feels himself at liberty to surround himself and family with accommodations rather more numerous and costly when grown rich, than he thought necessary or

---

2. In the early 1830s, many Baptist churches, including First Baptist in Charleston, were embroiled in battles over whether or not to allow musical instruments in their worship services. Manly and his son, Basil, Jr., worked long and hard to publish *The Baptist Psalmody*, a hymnal based on sound doctrine. For more on this, see Fuller, *Chaplain to the Confederacy*, 94–95, 210–211.

proper to him in the beginning of his fortune (and I see nothing in Scripture that condemns this, provided a due regard be paid to the simplicity and sobriety and benevolence of the Christian character), it would appear by parity of reasoning, since there are no express provisions in Scripture on the subject, that a congregation might consult their circumstances in a pecuniary point of view.... As a Christian individual would feel himself at liberty to derive his accommodations only from the class of allowable things, so a Christian congregation should feel bound ...by the same principle.

...These considerations however will not affect any who have conscientious scruples against the admissibility of instrumental music.... [I]s there anything in Scripture which...will make it improper [to introduce] instrumental music into the worship of the church?...

There is nothing wrong in instrumental music *in itself* nor with respect to the worship of God in a general point of view. Its allowed use in the *families of the pious*, *in the public worship of God* under a former dispensation, and the images employed in Revelation 5:8, 9; 14:2, concerning the Heavenly worship, plainly show that there is nothing *intrinsically* wrong in it.

...[I]n respect to its admissibility, [instrumental music] cannot be denied on any principle of Scripture or sound reason.... It is a thing indifferent, in itself, whether it be used or not used. Christian churches may do very well without it, and if they should have it, in the sober, legitimate use, they are not, on that account, the worse.

First Baptist Church of Charleston, South Carolina

(Original Architect's Drawing by Robert Mills. Courtesy
First Baptist Church, Charleston, South Carolina)

7

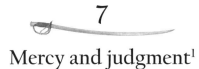

Mercy and judgment[1]

I will sing of mercy, and judgment,
unto thee, O Lord, will I sing.
—Psalm 101:1

This Psalm is thought to have been occasioned by the restoration of the Ark of God to its place, after it had been in possession of the enemies of Israel.... We may observe,

1. The resolution of the Psalmist —"I will sing." Music seems to be a natural language, adapted to the expression of what is joyous or mournful.... The Psalmist resolves to employ his highest powers in an act of grateful recollection and praise....

2. The subject of his song—"Mercy and judgment." Mercy is his benevolence to sinners; judgment relates to his character as a Sovereign or Judge, and is applied

---

1. Basil Manly, Sr., *Mercy and Judgment: A Discourse Containing Some Fragments of the History of the Baptist Church in Charleston, S.C. Delivered by Request of the Corporation of Said Church, September 23rd and 30th, A.D. 1832* (Charleston, S.C.: Knowles, Vose, 1837), *passim*. For a modern history of this church, see Robert A. Baker, Paul John Craven, Jr., and Robert Marshall Blalock, *History of the First Baptist Church, Charleston, South Carolina, 1682–2007* (Springfield, Mo.: Particular Baptist Press, 2007).

generally to those acts of God which are mysterious and afflictive. If we sing altogether of *mercy*, we may be wanting in reverence and godly fear. If we sing only of *judgment*, we may be deficient in gratitude. Mercy and judgment, either mingled or alternate, make up the history of our lives, fill the records of churches and of States; and both, therefore, should have appropriate part in all our celebrations.

3. The Auditor of the Song—"Unto thee, O Lord, will I sing." ...[A]ll acts of worship, public or private, should be done as to the Lord; that our minds should be so riveted on him, as present with us, and the object of our worship, that we should comparatively, and for the time, disregard all surrounding objects, and be singly occupied with the design of pleasing the ear of Jehovah.... Ah brethren! Our attention will be fixed, at least one day.

4. His object—that he might prepare and stimulate himself for the execution of his high trust, as well as express the overflowing feelings of his heart. From all which it would appear that the following sentiment is breathed in the text, viz. *That the grateful record of divine dispensations is a great help to duty. It furnishes direction.... It imposes restraints.... It supplies a most powerful motive.... It promotes perseverance....* And it reveals...that all desirable success and enjoyment are entirely dependent on God's delight in his people, and his blessing upon them....

These reflections are not an unsuitable comment on the occasion, *the celebration of the 150th Anniversary of our Church*, and may introduce a *sketch of its history*....

It has to be regretted, however, that the Church has no records to direct our enquiries; a series of calamities having deprived them of nearly every vestige of their own progress.... [On September 15, 1752, a] dreadful hurricane and inundation...visited [and]...the south-west corner of the Baptist Meeting House was carried away...and all the books and papers perished in the flood.... About thirty years after, on January 3, 1782, the British troops visited... and...they took, and either carried off or destroyed, "the old book kept by the Trustees...and also all the indents, acts, papers...of the church."[2]

The records and papers...were again destroyed, in the conflagration which consumed...the house of...the Church Clerk, in the year 1819. Thus the water, the fire, and the hand of the enemy, each in its turn, have deprived the Church of the means of relating its own history. Some printed documents, however, remain, and some papers preserved....

The Baptist Church in Charleston, S[outh] C[arolina], owes its origin to some of the mysterious, but wise dispensations of Providence, in which mercy and judgment are blended....

In the...year, 1656, [some English Baptist]...churches [in the West Country of England] published "A confession of the faith"...subscribed by twenty-five persons, ministers and laymen, in behalf of the whole.[3] Among these names is *William Screven*, of *Somerton*. This is the individual...who afterwards became the honored founder of this church. Driven by persecution, or impelled by those

---

2. This was during the American Revolution.

3. *A Confession of the Faith of Several Churches of Christ* (London, 1656), known as the Somerset Confession.

motives which lead good men to emigrate, he left his native land for America.... In 1681...we find him settled at Kittery,... Maine—and employed in holding religious meetings in his own house.... [The persecution of the Baptists by the Puritans of New England, though, forced him and his flock to flee to South Carolina.]....[4]

We, who live in these times of universal toleration, are astonished that men, professing godliness, should have been guilty of such absurd, cruel, and unchristian proceedings. But we are not to suppose that therefore they were all bad men. This part of their conduct surely was an error. But their error was that of the times in which they lived.... Although they had fled from the old world to enjoy liberty of conscience in the new, it was not against spiritual tyranny, in itself, they objected, but against its bearing on themselves. They still cherished a notion of the right of the civil magistrate to interfere in religious concerns, and labored as much to secure uniformity in the modes of worship in the new world, as their oppressors had done in the old. Happy are we who live at a period when the principles of civil and religious liberty are better understood....

No sooner were the Baptists settled in their new place of worship, than they began to seek after their spiritual

---

4. William Screven (1629-1713)—his name is sometimes spelled Scriven or Screeven—led the Baptist work he pastored in Kittery, Maine, to migrate wholesale to Charleston, South Carolina, in 1696. At the time of this migration, Screven was sixty-seven. Over the next few years, God owned his labors. Of a population of 4,180 in and around Charleston by 1708, it is estimated that 10% were Baptist.

establishment on the foundation of the doctrines of grace. Simultaneously with the erection of the building, they sent to England for copies of "A confession of the faith of more than a hundred congregations of Christians...in London and the country, in 1689," called the *Century* Confession.[5] This they carefully examined and adopted verbatim in the year 1700, as the confession of this Church; and so it has remained to this day.

But while they were thus careful to secure among them soundness in the faith, they were no less "careful to maintain good works." Animated with the spirit and guided by the example of Mr. Screven, who at the age of more than "three score years and ten," was still the laborious missionary, they procured ministers, and some among themselves who had the gift of exhortation, to go into the surrounding settlements, and preach the everlasting Gospel....

The Church in Charleston, diminished in numbers, and reduced in strength...was now destined to undergo a series of the severest trials.... Just in this gloomy crisis, however, it pleased God by the ministry of Mr. [George] Whitefield,[6] to revive his work; in the fruits of which the Baptists largely shared, and many joined them.... The Lord had provided an instrument by which he designed greatly to promote the cause of truth and piety in the province, in the person of the Rev. Oliver Hart, [who was deeply influ-

---

5. Second London Confession (1689).

6. The evangelistic tours of George Whitefield (1714–1770) in America during the 1740s were central to the Great Awakening. He was in America in 1738, 1739–1741, and 1744–1748.

enced by the ministry of George Whitefield].... It pleased
God to arrest him early by his grace, and bring him to the
knowledge of truth.[7]

...Mr. Hart's preaching attracted considerable attention in Charleston, and his character, universal respect....
While his great end in life was the glory of God, he viewed
the salvation of sinners as a principal means of promoting it. He longed for the souls of men.... The church now
enjoyed a steady season of peace and prosperity, while
Mr. Hart continued to grow in the affection and esteem
of all parties.[8]

...[On] the 18th of October, 1787, [Richard Furman
became the pastor].[9] ...No man more fully appreciated the
particular obligations of the pastoral relation than did Dr.
Furman: yet he was not insensible to the claims of missionary labor.... His labor was not in vain in the Lord...

---

7. On Oliver Hart (1723–1795), see Loulie Latimer Owens, *Oliver
Hart 1723–1795. A Biography* (Greenville, S.C.: South Carolina Baptist
Historical Society, 1966), 3. This biographical study can also be found
in *Baptist History and Heritage*, 1, no. 2 (July, 1966): 19–46. See also Richard Furman, *Rewards of Grace conferred on Christ's Faithful People: A Sermon
occasioned by the decease of the Rev. Oliver Hart, A.M.* (Charleston, 1796).

8. Hart was compelled by the British invasion of Charleston, during the American Revolution, to leave his church in 1780. He found his
way to Hopewell, New Jersey, and became the pastor of the Baptist
church there, never to return to Charleston.

9. On Furman, see James A. Rogers, *Richard Furman: Life and Legacy*
(Macon, Ga.: Mercer University Press, 1985) and Zaqueu Moreira de
Oliveira, "Richard Furman, Father of the Southern Baptist Conven-
tion," in *The Lord's Free People in a Free Land. Essays in Baptist History in honor
of Robert A. Baker*, ed. William R. Estep (Fort Worth: Southwestern
Baptist Theological Seminary, 1976), 87–98.

[and he worked] to refresh the spirits of God's destitute people, in the regions through which he passed.

...January 17, 1822, the new building was first opened for worship, and dedicated to the service of Almighty God, with a sermon from the Rev. Dr. Furman.... Shortly after this enlargement of the accommodations of worship, the hearts of the members were also enlarged. While the church had enjoyed a steady onward progress all through the ministry of Dr. Furman, various seasons of refreshing had occurred at intervals;...and it now pleased God to raise up a goodly number of willing converts....

But the time drew near when the servant of the Lord should die.... [To members of his congregation who came to visit him on his deathbed,] he would, faltering, say, "I am a dying man; but my trust is in the Redeemer. I preach Christ to you, dying, as I have attempted to do whilst living: I commend Christ and his salvation to you." ...He died on the night of the 25th of August, A.D. 1825. *Farewell — Farewell —Thou Man of God!*

James C. Furman (1809–1891)

8

The need for a Southern Baptist Theological Seminary

Letter from Basil Manly, Sr., to James Furman[1]

Charleston, S.C., February 26, 1835

My dear brother

…The [Theological] Institution is indeed a matter of engrossing moment…. The truth is, Georgia, North Carolina, Tennessee and South Carolina ought to be one in this business, and if we take our measures wisely it will result in that. The schools in Georgia and North Carolina, though flourishing, have failed wholly as Theological Institutions. The friends of them have given them up in that view. We must now make a Theological School, on the manual labour plan, gradually raising the standard of attainment in it, place it in a cheap part of the country, not liable to objections from our neighbouring states, and it

1. Basil Manly, Sr., to James C. Furman, February 26, 1835, in *The Life and Work of James Clement Furman*, ed. Harvey Toliver Cook (Greenville, S.C.: Alester G. Furman, 1826), 42–43. James C. Furman was the son of the late Richard Furman. Manly first tried a plan of cooperation among the Southern states for the support of the theological institution at Furman in 1830. He and other agents worked hard to raise the funds to support the school, but the plan failed. For more on this, see Fuller, *Chaplain to the Confederacy*, 80–81.

will inevitably draw the best students from them.... Turn these things in your mind and let us hear your views.

Affectionately,

B. Manly

"Theological education in the Southern States"[2]

Charleston, S.C. March 11, 1835

Mr. Editor,

...You are aware that by various bodies in this State, and the adjoining States of North Carolina and Georgia, some experiments have been made in the great enterprise of training the minds of our young Ministers to the capacity of more elevated and extended usefulness. The result has been to increase our sense of its importance; but it is questionable whether the principles on which it should be conducted are yet settled or understood. It is perhaps incident to every great undertaking, that its commencement should exhibit the mistakes of inexperience, and the consequent waste of time and strength — and indeed, it seems to be a part of the plan of Divine Providence, that every good institution should grow up amid solicitudes and disappointments, and attain its usefulness by the nurture of prayers and tears and anxious labours....

With relation to the present subject, the great question to be first disposed of is, How shall the means of suitable instruction be provided? A Theological School, in respect of its funds, does not stand on the footing of

---

2. Basil Manly, Sr., "Theological Education in the Southern States," *Southern Baptist and General Intelligencer* (March 13, 1835): 170–172.

common schools. In them, those who receive instruction pay the price, and thus they are sustained. But it pleases God to order, that the great mass of those who are entering the Ministry, should be unable to do this; or if they were universally able even to pay ordinary tuition rates, the number is too small, or too fluctuating, and the kind of instruction too varied and extensive to allow such a provision to be adequate.

To meet the demands of the case, therefore, different expedients have been resorted to. In one case, it is has been attempted to raise a sufficient sum by annual subscriptions to supply the place of tuition money. The inequality of collections, and the difficulty, uncertainty, and expense of making them is an insuperable objection to this method. It would be injustice to competent instructors to invite them to rely on so precarious a support, after the experience already had.

In other cases, Theological Schools have attempted to avail themselves of the general love of learning, to draw together a number of youth preparing for the ordinary vocations of life, who, paying the price of their instruction, would support teachers capable of superintending theological studies with a portion of their time. This has been attempted in each of the States mentioned. In this State, it was found inexpedient, and abandoned some years ago. As to the issue of the experiments now under progress in our sister States, perhaps it would be assuming in any but one of themselves, to pronounce a decided opinion. Relative to the general plan, however, we may be permitted to make our observations freely. It is subject to the inconvenience of associating ill-instructed *young men* with well-taught *boys* in the same institution and pursuits and exposing the former to the mortification and injury of degrading comparisons. But what is worse, it leaves to those, who ought to be chiefly regarded, but a fragment of the time and attention of their instructors. It is right that they who pay the price should receive an equivalent benefit. The ordinary students cannot be neglected or postponed; else, either injustice is done to them, or their patronage, which supports the school, is withdrawn. The Theological students, therefore, can receive only that measure of attention which may be entirely consistent with the ordinary operations and success of the classical department. The obvious and inevitable effect is to make that department *superior*, the other *subordinate*, and in proportion to the success and reputation of the school in general, will be the depression of the interests of the Theological department. The tendency will constantly be toward the absorption of the one by the other; and it cannot be reciprocal, it swallows up itself, and both will fail together....

It is not intended as a reproach to our young brethren, to say that many of them, when they first come to study, are not able to spell half the words they are required to use; some of them cannot legibly write their names; while others have had a collegiate education, and need to be inducted into all the depths and intricacies of sacred learning. Let us suppose thirty young men [were] placed together, under all the varieties of attainment indicated by these extremes. Is it too much to demand that the whole time of Instructors be given to them? They have not time to spend in waiting for instruction at the occasional and ill-adapted lessons of ordinary schools. They are wanted in their Master's service with the least possible delay of preparation. Each individual of them must, in some respects, constitute a separate class; must have his education conducted in reference to his own age, capacity, state of advancement or deficiency, and other circumstances *peculiar to himself*; and all made to bear directly on the sacred work for which he is destined. How is it possible that this can be done in an institution where this class of students is necessarily subordinate, and reduced by uncontrollable circumstances to a fragment of their teaching time? And I would enquire, with all deference and kindness, of our brethren who know the state of things in the Wake Forest and Mercer Institutes, whether they do not find, in spite of themselves, that the theological is merged in the classical department? Is it not true to a great extent, that the money given by Baptists and their friends to provide liberal facilities for the *benefit of young ministers, must needs be* diverted in the mixed institution, for its principle design; and employed rather for the benefit of the sons of gentlemen, who are much better able to form schools for themselves, than the Baptists are for them? This circumstance is not to be imputed to individuals as blameworthy. It results, not from wrong motives, or from negligence or unfaithfulness; but from the necessary operation of such a plan. And I confess I am unable to see how it can admit of a corrective. My opinion is that the plan itself is radically defective, and will have to be abandoned in other States, as it has in this. Those respectable and useful institutions will naturally resolve themselves into seminaries of our sons promiscuously — while the wants of the denomination in reference to young ministers will remain to be provided for in some other way. Should this result ensue, the labor bestowed in rearing them will not be lost. Such institutions are much needed in all the States, and must sooner or later be formed. Our brethren have gone ahead of us, and we must bring up the rear. There will be no want of means for their establishment; whatever other interest may flourish or fail, those of liberal education will continue to advance. Each generation will be more learned than that which preceded it: and in contributing to found schools for common education under religious auspices, we not only provide a rich inheritance for our children, but place ourselves among the benefactors of mankind.

But still, what we want beyond all this, is an Institution suitably furnished and endowed for the *exclusive benefit* of those who are entering upon the ministry of the Word. Such an Institution must not be confined to a single State. What *might be done* by the denomination of any State, is not the question. They might do much; as in each of the Southern States they are, as a body, numerous and wealthy. But there is no reason to suppose that any State will do more for some time than to endow one professorship, and put a competent salary beyond the reach of ordinary contingency. This, it is true, would be doing something. A school would then be established, and though its means of instruction would be limited, they would be certain and permanent. This can be done soon for the Furman Theological Institution — if the various bodies in S[outh] C[arolina] holding funds for education purposes, perceiving the true interests of the denomination, should put them all together in a permanent fund, pledged exclusively to the support of a Theological Professor. And this, I sincerely hope, will be done....

What is wanted, however, is that North Carolina and Georgia should each do the same thing, adopt a common site, and a name for the Institution, suitable to them all — should establish a board of trustees, consisting of an equal number from each State, to administer the affairs of the Institution — which being thus furnished with three well endowed Professors, would be reputable, and adequate to all the demands of the Denomination in the Southern States. If all the available funds now collected in each State should be exhausted in accomplishing this result, it would be a service to the *cause* of education. It would be a rallying point and a stimulus, now so much wanted. There being no more money wanted for salaries, all the [energies] of our churches and friends could be turned to the single object of assisting beneficiaries. Connected with these individually, there would always be personal considerations and motives to benevolence, sufficient to relieve the general fund, either in whole or in part — and their expenses might be further reduced by a prudent system of economical arrangement, and by the aid of *regular manual labor, as a necessary part of the plan of education.* In short, we have sketched the outline of a plan for a great Southern Baptist Institution, which would grow and expand itself under the divine blessing, into an importance and usefulness which we cannot now conceive. Our more sagacious brethren of the Northern and Middle States are giving up their separate action, and uniting in the conjoined cause…. All parties among the friends of education there, after years of fruitless or meagre experiment, are led to coalesce for the common good; and the result is most salutary. Shall we not profit by their experience? What is to hinder the Baptists of the Carolinas and Georgia from being one in this important enterprise? What, but their own unwise policy? There is a point near the Tennessee border, where the three States so nearly converge, that a common site might be selected, equally convenient to them all—and there can be no contest of location. That State will conceive of itself most honored that yields the point for the general good.

I beseech my brethren of these States to take the subject under serious and prayerful consideration…. I invite the free expression of views, through our respective papers, from all my brethren—and more than all, *I would respectfully propose that measures be taken to have a convention of the friends of this cause from the Carolinas and Georgia, and such other Southern and Western States as may be disposed to unite with them, to assemble at some central point to deliberate and form some united plan for the accomplishment of this great object.*

I remain, dear brother, yours most truly,

— B. Manly

9

The whipping of Sam

Diary Entry, March 11, 1839[1]

> College Servant, Sam. Monday, March 11, 1839. This day a servant by the name of Sam came to me by order of the Governor to be tried as a servant for the University. I set him to work immediately.

Diary Entry, March 4, 1846 [2]

> This afternoon, the college boy, Sam, behaved very insolently to Thomas G. Green; and refused to measure or receive a load of coal which Green had brought. By order of the Faculty he was chastised in

---

1. Basil Manly, Sr., "Diary II (1834–1846)," p. 144 (March 11, 1839), Manly Family Papers, William Stanley Hoole Special Collections Library, University of Alabama, Tuscaloosa.

2. Basil Manly, Sr., "Record Book I (1843–1848)," p. 65 (March 4, 1846), Manly Family Papers, William Stanley Hoole Special Collections Library, University of Alabama, Tuscaloosa. The incident described in this entry became a central part of the argument over whether or not the University of Alabama should apologize for slavery, which it did in 2004. For more on the controversy over the university's apology, see Alfred L. Brophy, "The University and the Slaves: Apology and Its

my room, in their presence. Not seeming humbled, I whipped him a second time, very severely.

Diary Entry, February 11, 1850 [3]

The Faculty this day resolved that they will sell Sam, the college servant. This college servant has been here since March 11, 1839. He has always been impudent and hard to manage. It now appears that he was very impudent and insubordinate to [one of the professors] on Saturday last. All things taken into account, the Faculty thought it best to sell him…. [Sam was sold and sent to his new owner on Tuesday, February 12, 1850.]

Diary Entry, February 16, 1850 [4]

On Saturday, February 16, Sam came to me overwhelmed with grief, begging to be taken back….

Meaning," in *The Age of Apology: Facing Up to the Past*, ed. Mark Gibney and Rhoda E. Howard-Hassmann (Philadelphia: University of Pennsylvania Press, 2008), 109–119.

3. Basil Manly, Sr., "Record Book II (1848–1855)," pp. 62–63 (February 11, 1850), Manly Family Papers, William Stanley Hoole Special Collections Library, University of Alabama, Tuscaloosa.

4. Manly, Sr, "Record Book II (1848–1855)," p. 63 (February 16, 1850).

Diary Entry, February 18, 1850 [5]

At the Faculty meeting on Monday, Sam's case was brought up by [a professor] who expressed the belief that he is truly penitent; and when distinctly asked, he further said that he prefers to have Sam reinstated, whereupon the Faculty rescinded the order to sell Sam.... My private opinion is that he should be sold, as a matter of policy. But, so far as anything that I have to order or require from Sam is concerned, I am not afraid that he will disobey or displease me, personally, in any serious degree.

5. Manly, Sr, "Record Book II (1848–1855)," p. 63 (February 18, 1850).

John L. Dagg (1794–1884)

10

Thoughts on slavery

Letter from Basil Manly, Sr., to George Barton Ide, Philadelphia[1]

University of Alabama, August 27, 1844

Rev. Sir,

My friend and brother…has just informed me…of some remarks of yours in relation to me before a committee of the late Triennial Convention, intended to sustain your objections to my nomination as an officer of that body.[2] Since the spring of 1836, I have occasionally seen and heard of those allegations, about selling a negro as I would a horse, etc. and hitherto I have not thought it worthwhile… to vindicate myself.…I should be disposed to suffer in

---

1. Basil Manly, Sr., to George Barton Ide in Basil Manly, Sr., "Diary II (1834–1846)," pp. 321–325 (August 27, 1844). George Barton Ide (1804–1872) was a Baptist minister originally from Vermont and prominent in Northern Baptist circles.

2. Founded in 1814, the Triennial Convention was a national organization of American Baptists for the purpose of foreign missions. When the convention refused to accept James E. Reeve of Georgia as a missionary in 1844 because he was a slave owner, the Baptists in the South formed the Southern Baptist Convention. Basil Manly, Sr., played a key role in the secession of the Southern Baptists.

silence, not in the haughty disdain usually imputed to Southern slaveholders, but simply under the Christian feeling that such things are part of the bitter herbs put up with our provision for our journey through the wilderness, and on the principle which induced David to say, "Let him curse, for perhaps the Lord hath bidden him." 2 Samuel 16:10. As for office in the Convention, I regard it not: I should still do all I could for the cause of missions, in some way, had I been left out. As to a desire to cultivate a better understanding with certain of my northern brethren,... I see reason why so much respect and toleration, at least, should be felt, as would enable all parties to cooperate in the great objects and enterprises of our union. Because I now see this union seriously threatened, and to leave no share of the blame of a separation on myself, I am willing to obtrude on your attention, in a good spirit, I hope, an explanation and history of facts which no considerations merely personal to myself could draw to me.

Be it known, then, that my father in North Carolina was the owner of some 25 slaves at his death. These belonged wholly to one family. His children,... looked on these negroes with something more than a feeling of humanity, a feeling of attachment and friendship. We divided them out among us, by agreement, as *they* saw best inclined with the feeling that none of us would part from them without an imperious and uncontrollable necessity. One of these accompanied me to Charleston and was a kind of confidential servant, became exceedingly capable and valuable, as a cook, house servant, body servant, and coach-man. He was treated with great indulgence, he ate the same that I did, wore clothes as good as mine, was lodged comfortably, and was not uninstructed in the things of religion. But the negroes of a wealthy neighbor corrupted him; he became a gambler, fond of drink, exceedingly dissolute, and even diseased; and was fast verging to ruin. I reasoned with him; when that would not do, I chastised him. This was repeated a time or two in the course of a few months and was done by my own hands in private, and to avoid the exposure and consequent recklessness of sending him to the work-house. I, at last, told him that I would whip him but once more; that, if he could not be reclaimed, I could not keep him; and would not have the peace of my life disturbed by the continual and painful anxiety of having to chastise him, as he was now nearly grown. It was not long before he again transgressed, (gaming away his clothes and being out to the neglect of his necessary business); and when he found that I knew it, he ran away. *The first and only time that ever a servant of mine avoided my presence.* When I recovered him, he begged so hard that I could not sell him, and my other servants joining the entreaty, I consented to try him again. I told him [that] I could not consent to have so vicious a person in a confidential relation about my house, that he might select his business, and I would put him to it, and would still be his owner and friend if he would behave so that I possibly could. He chose the trade of carpenter and I put him to [a] humane man that worked with his hands. After a considerable lapse of time, I found that he would be absent from his employer for a day or two at a time, excuse himself on his return by saying that he was sick and under the doctor's hands at my house, where he still slept; but meanwhile he would be skulking about the city indulging in various forms of sin. I was determined not to chastise him again, so I took him soberly to me, kindly pointed out to him all the consequences of his course both as to this world and the next, and told him that [he] must now consider himself on his last probation, and that I should sell him on the next proof he gave me that he did not mean to reform. A few months only passed before I found him habitually devoted to vices, *new* and *old*, and becoming so corrupt as to be wholly intolerable. I therefore put him into the hands of a factor, and directed he should be sold. The necessity of this measure had been deeply deplored. I had used every measure I knew of to avoid it, under the feeling before described. But when it became unavoidable, I did it firmly and without flinching.

This happened in...1836 and, soon after, I went to Hartford, [Connecticut, on church business].... From Hartford, I went to Boston, in pursuance of private business, where I saw you. The Reverend Henry Jackson was then a pastor in Charleston, Massachusetts. His wife...[and] her sisters...had spent months together in my house in Charleston, and for several successive years. My house, indeed, was like a home to them, and not only my servants, but my wife was their slave.... But everything we could do for the children...was a pleasure to us. And we never tired under the exertions and sacrifices which hospitality seemed to require.

[In Massachusetts,] Mr. Jackson...proposed we should ride to [visit a fellow minister]. To this I consented (I paid for the horse and chaise).... We were out all day and his attention seemed absorbed in questioning me, in the most unrestrained manner, about all the peculiarities of Southern society, institutions, and manners. Suspecting nothing but friendship, I gave my whole mind to him, told him freely everything he asked about, however curious, or prying he might have been. Among other things that much excited his curiosity was the whole condition of slavery. He asked me how many slaves I had, what their ages, how they were treated, if I had ever bought or sold one, and so on, endlessly. I bore it all, and answered all, in the simplicity and kindness of my heart, and took occasion, as we were riding alone, to narrate the circumstances of my then recent trial in respect to that boy. I remember him asking me if it were really the feeling at the South that we had a right to sell them at will. I told him, it certainly was; that however great the trial was to my feelings in other respects, I had none as to the right of property in him; and that, in that particular, I had no more doubt or compunction than in pocketing the price of a horse or anything else that belonged to me.

...As to the information alleged to depend on the declarations "of a highly respectable lady, who had lived in Tuskaloosa," this is news indeed. I scarcely know how to treat it. Were a gentleman your informant, and I a worldly man, I suppose you know how a Southern man would treat it.[3] But I have no haughty, no angry, nor vindictive

---

3. Manly implies that a worldly Southerner would challenge Ide to a duel.

feelings.... I should never have adverted to it, nor made
an inquiry as to the author...but for the disturbed state of
relations between the North and the South, as to a common cause, dear to the Christian heart. In view of this...I
respectfully and kindly, but earnestly and solemnly,... ask
you to inform me, on whose authority it was you made the
statement before the committee (about my alleged "common habit of going out, taking off my coat, and severely
whipping every servant about my premises, just for the
pleasure of the exercise.") What was it the person said,
exactly, and to whom? Surely, no circumstances of deli-
cacy or duty can require you to keep secret the author of
a falsehood so injurious, especially when you are willing
to make use of it yourself.... If I should be disappointed
in obtaining an explicit and full answer, will you answer
this question? Was it Mrs. Dagg, the wife of my esteemed
friend and brother, the Rev. J. L. Dagg, now of Penfield,
Georgia? I expect, however, no concealment or evasion.[4]

In hope of eternal life, through unsearchable riches of
grace,
                              — B. Manly

---

4. Mrs. Dagg was the wife of John L. Dagg, a Virginia native who
was a noted Baptist theologian, minister, and president of Mercer University. Ide did not respond to this letter but eventually responded to
another by indicating that Mrs. Dagg was his source. Manly wrote to
John Dagg about it, but the situation was left unresolved. He came to
believe that Ide had twisted a few rumors in order to attack Manly
and slavery in general. Manly's honor had been slighted and he felt
he had to respond. For all of this, see Fuller, *Chaplain to the Confederacy*,
222–223.

11

Divine efficiency consistent with human activity[1]

> *Work out your own salvation, with fear and trembling;*
> *for it is God that worketh in you, both to will and to do,*
> *of his good pleasure.*
>   —Philippians 2:12–13

…[This] could not mean, by working out our own salvation, *devising the plan*—that is the Father's work, and was
done long ago. Not *redemption or justification*—these were
the Son's work, and were accomplished in that one offer-

---

1. Basil Manly, Sr., *Divine Efficiency Consistent with Human Activity:
Notes of a Sermon Delivered by Rev. Basil Manly, D.D., at Pleasant Grove Church,
Fayette Co., Alabama, April 8th, 1849* (Tuscaloosa: M. D. J. Slade, 1849),
7–16, *passim.* Manly was asked to deliver this sermon during a period of
theological controversy among Alabama Baptists. Some churches had
embraced the Arminian doctrine of free will, while the majority held
fast to Calvinism and the doctrines of grace. The sermon was given at a
conference designed to reconcile the two camps and was so successful
that it was widely praised and circulated.

The full sermon can also be found in *Southern Baptist Sermons on
Sovereignty and Responsibility* (Harrisonburg, Va.: Gano Books / Sprinkle
Publications, 1984), 7–32. See also http://www.geocities.com/baptist_
documents/1849.cl.al.manly.work.out.html.

ing, completed when he said "it is *finished*,"[2] and went to plead that finished sacrifice before the throne of God. Not regeneration—that is the Spirit's work, and is evidently supposed to have been already wrought in those very persons. They were saved saints—so far, therefore, as regards regeneration, and sanctification, (in part at least,) salvation was already wrought in them.

What, then, is it? It seems to be the yielding of the mind to the motions of the Spirit, when once it has been renewed…by the Lord. It includes all the duties of practical piety, in the widest sense. It is the power of God which…implants the life. It is the duty of men to use the means to develop the seminal principle implanted within them.… [T]he Christian is to work out his own salvation, by cultivating the principle of grace, and conducting it through all the different stages of growth and Christian experience.…

This interpretation is consistent with the scheme of salvation, since it harmonizes freedom and the power of choice in man, with the sovereignty and antecedent grace of God.…

1. This idea grows, naturally and necessarily, out of our dependent condition as creatures. That all creatures are dependent is obvious both from reason and Scripture. "In him we live, and move, and have our being."[3] If God cease to propel the vital current through our veins, to heave the

---

2. John 19:30.
3. Acts 17:28.

breast, and give motion to the organs of life, we sink, we perish, we fill the silent tomb. In regard, specially, to all that is spiritual, it is true, also, that "our sufficiency is of God"....

2. Both truths together, that men act and are acted upon, seem to be included in the general fact that all holy exercises are both commanded as a duty, and promised as a gift. Faith is the key of all the other graces, the commencement and token of all the rest. It is, accordingly, commanded, and put as if for the whole. "Believe on the Lord Jesus Christ and thou shalt be saved." "He that believeth not is condemned already; because he hath not believed on the only begotten Son of God."[4]....

Repentance: "Repent ye, therefore, and be converted, that your sins may be blotted out." "God now commands all men everywhere to repent." But Christ is exalted "to give repentance and remission of sins."[5]

Regeneration, which includes so large a part of experimental religion: In the Old Testament, God commands, "make you a new heart;" yet, he says, "a new heart will I give you."[6] The same thing is expressed by *quickening*: that God quickens us, is written over the whole Bible; but we are commanded to "awake...and arise from the dead."[7] The *new Creation* is the subject of similarly blended com-

---

4. Acts 16:31; John 3:18.

5. Acts 3:19; 17:30; 5:31 (Manly has modified the last of these verses).

6. Ezekiel 18:31; 36:26.

7. Ephesians 5:14.

mands and promises: we are "created in Christ Jesus unto good works" and also exhorted to "put on the new man."[8]

Turning to God: "Turn us again, O Lord of Hosts!" Yet the command comes, "Let the wicked forsake his way, and the unrighteous man his thoughts; and let him return unto the Lord." "Turn ye, turn ye; why will ye die?"[9]

Love: If there is anything that would seem to be purely a matter of Christian duty, it is love. "Love the Lord, all ye his saints."[10] "Take good heed therefore *unto yourselves*, that ye love the Lord your God," Joshua 23:11. Yet, this same love is "shed abroad in our hearts by the Holy Ghost which is given unto us," Romans 5:5.

Coming to Christ: "Come, for all things are now ready," says the Savior, stretching his bounteous hands, and inviting the hungry, and weary, and ruined. Yet, this same compassionate Savior says, "No man can come unto me, except the Father which hath sent me draw him."[11]

Perseverance in holiness: That this is a Christian duty need not be argued. But it is God that both *begins* and *performs* the good work in his people, Philippians 1:6. That this passage relates to perseverance in holiness is obvious from the whole connexion.

3. Commands and petitions are mingled all through the Scriptures; and...prove that men both act, and are acted upon, by a divine operation. Commands prove that men

---

8. Ephesians 2:10; 4:24.
9. Psalm 80:19; Isaiah 55:7; Ezekiel 33:11.
10. Psalm 31:23.
11. Luke 14:17; John 6:44.

act—for, when God says *do any thing*, it implies that men are not stocks, not stones, but moral agents—capable of moral suasion, of understanding and acting, upon motives freely. Prayers, on the other hand, suppose that God acts on us—and that he both can, and will, work in us; both to will and to do....

Let us not, then, give up either the doctrine of human activity and responsibility, or that of the divine sovereignty and efficiency....

The Scriptures do not undertake to explain mysteries. They leave them unexplained. There is a difference between difficulties, and mysteries—difficulties may be removed—mysteries cannot, without a new revelation, or the bestowment of a higher intellect....

The greatest reason, however, why the Christian family is divided on one or the other side—rejecting one or the other of these great doctrines—is that the doctrine of dependence on the Divine Being, throws us constantly into the hands, and on the mercy of God. Proud man does not like it; prefers to look at the other side of the subject; becomes blinded, in part, by gazing at one view of the truth, alone; and forgets the Maker, in whom he lives, and moves and has his being.[12]

The Scriptures, in no ambiguous manner, intimate the true reply to this question. We are confident that "*he that hath begun* a good work in you will perform it, etc." "Draw me; we will run after thee."[13] I will not multiply quotations;

---

12. See Acts 17:28.
13. Philippians 1:6; Song of Songs 1:4.

the current of scripture ascribes the incipient operation to God. "I have loved thee with an everlasting love; therefore with loving-kindness have I drawn thee." "Ye have not chosen me, but I have chosen you, and ordained you, that ye should go and bring forth fruit." "Of his own will begat he us with the word of truth." "No man can come to me, except the Father which hath sent me draw him." "Which were born not of blood, nor of the will of the flesh, nor of the will of man, but of God."[14]

But how was it in your experience? Let us go back, in our consciousness, with this question: for, if there is a work of grace in us, that work is a subject of consciousness, to some extent. Now I ask any Christian man to say — Did you go, irrespective of motive, go *first* to meet him and then he came to meet you? Did you, without a change of heart, resolve to change your own heart? And did this effort, self-determined, self-sustained, self-dependent, succeed?

If so, the credit of the whole operation, the merit of the work, belongs to you. The Christian heart replies, no, Jesus sought me first. I remember a pious old Methodist Lady, singing with my Mother, that hymn "Come thou fount of every blessing,"[15] and when she reached the verse "Jesus sought me when a stranger, wandering from the fold of God," she burst into tears, and hid her face in her handkerchief, and said, "Yes, it was so, it was so."

There spoke the true Christian heart. Take a true

---

14. Jeremiah 31:3; John 15:16; James 1:18; John 6:44; 1:13.

15. A well-known hymn by the Baptist hymnwriter and minister Robert Robinson (1735–1790).

believer away from theological creeds and technicalities, from the musty volumes of controversy and the arena of bitter strife, and there is but one voice on the subject: "Not unto us, not unto us, but unto God be *all* the glory."[16]

How began that work, and who began it? Oh! if I had a tongue that could alarm the dead in their narrow house — and, for an audience the assembled universe — I would rejoice to shout the acclamations of Glory to their rightful object. It is all due to God who loved me first, and gave himself for me, who, when I was guiltily disinclined to it, brought my unwilling heart to seek him. Then, and thus, it began; hence, it is of grace, not of works....

My brethren, however mysterious and incomprehensible it may be, that God chose a poor sinner like me — freely chose me, loved me, redeemed me, called me, justified me, and will glorify me — I will rejoice in the truth, and thank him for his free grace!

─────────────

16. See Psalm 115:1.

12

Divine efficiency consistent with human activity:
Some concluding words[1]

I will now endeavor to gather up some fragments of thought suggested by this great subject, and press them on your attention.

1. *It grows out of this doctrine that men's actions are their own....* God may work in us to will and to do; but *we* will, *we* do. Faith is produced by His Spirit in our hearts, but *we* believe. He may produce the actions but the actions are ours. This cannot be altered or disguised.

Whether men act well or ill, their actions are their own. We are justly under the divine influences, in full possession of all that is necessary to moral agency. His divine operation does not take away the power of understanding, or the faculty of conscience, or the capacity to will, freely, in view of motives. These three things are the essentials to moral agency; understanding, to compre-

---

1. Basil Manly, Sr., *Divine Efficiency Consistent with Human Activity*, 16–21.

hend the nature of the action; conscience, to appreciate its moral quality; and will[,] to apprehend motives and choose freely, whether we shall do it or not. But none of these being taken away...by God's operation, the agent is fully a moral agent, and the acts are truly his own.

Unless it is admitted that Divine efficiency is consistent with human freedom and activity, it is obvious that there can be no holiness in the good actions of men, and no sinfulness in their evil actions; but the whole groundwork and foundation of morality will be overturned.

2. *Necessity in human action is not the same as compulsion.* If God works in us to will and to do, there is a necessity that we should will and do; but we are not *compelled* either to will or do. The act is obliged to be; but the man, in acting, is free.... In regard to salvation, so far from compelling a man, against his will, the very thing which God does is to make him willing to act right.... The Christian is willing, and chooses to do right; because a divine operation has made him so. He feels free; he is conscious that he is as heartily free in now trying to serve God, as when he went after the vanities and follies of his unconverted state.

3. *Sinners are free in working out their own destruction....* All God's arrangements of grace and invitations are directed, not with a view to damn, but to save; but men *may* work out their own damnation; and the responsibility is theirs. This, my brethren, is an awful subject.... Oh! what a result to take place, when listening to the word of God? Taking place now perhaps, with some of you who are doing

nothing more with the gracious instruments of good, than to turn them to self-destruction— as though a madman, drowning, should strangle himself with the rope thrown out to his assistance, and with his own hands complete his own destruction!

4. *God converts sinners in a way consistent with their moral freedom.* That it is God's work to convert a soul, let all Heaven and Earth, and every Saint, arise and proclaim. But, are not men free, in this also?... When we call on the sinner to repent, we feel that we are exhorting him to a duty; yet, if we have any sense or gospel in us, we do not mean that he either will, or can, do it without divine aid. The sinner knows that he is responsible. If he does not repent, he knows that it is his own fault. Our conscience, when we come to consider, convinces us of unbelief, not as a calamity, a misfortune; but a sin. How little excusable are you, when you do not come to Christ? You may do right—You may love God— choose life — walk the narrow way — you are required to do this; and are guilty and condemned for not doing it. The divine aid is, indeed, necessary to your doing it; but that aid is freely offered you....

5. *God is perfectly sincere in his counsels and invitations: notwithstanding his divine foreknowledge of the consequences.* That a God of Omniscience foresees that one person will repent, and that another will not, must be admitted by all. Yet, He offers mercy to all.

Jefferson Davis (1808–1889)

(Photo in National Archives, Washington, D.C.)

13

Praying for the confederate government

Diary Entries from February, 1861[1]

February 4, 1861

The Congress of the Seceding States met in Montgomery today.... [The officer presiding] called the meeting to order, and requested that R. W. Barnwell of S.C.[2] act as temporary chairman. On his taking the seat, he called on me to pray — which I tried to do.... [T]he President was requested to appoint a committee of 5, to present rules of the government of the body. The body then adjourned, till tomorrow noon. Thus has been inaugurated this important movement. May the Father of Lights guide the Whole!

---

1. Basil Manly, Sr., "Diary 4 (1858–1867)," pp. xxxvi–xxxvii (February 4, 9, 11, 18, 1861), Manly Family Papers, William Stanley Hoole Special Collections Library, University of Alabama, Tuscaloosa. For more on Manly's role as government chaplain, see Fuller, *Chaplain to the Confederacy*, 290–296.

2. Robert W. Barnwell (1801–1882) was a planter and prominent politician who had served in the U.S. Senate.

Saturday Morning, February 9

Last night, about 11 o'clock the Congress agreed, unanimously, upon a Constitution for the provisional Government of "*the Confederate States of America.*" It is substantially the Constitution of the United States, modified here and there so as to suit the Southern views of the rights of the States. The preamble invokes "the favor of Almighty God." This was inserted, I have no doubt, on a suggestion which came through [another minister] and myself. In the absence of the Methodist Episcopal Minister,...whose turn it was to open the Congress with Prayer, I was requested to perform that service, and did so. During the forenoon of Saturday, February 9, the Congress elected, unanimously, voting by states, Jefferson Davis of Mississippi, President, and Alexander H. Stephens of Georgia, Vice President, of this Provisional Government of these Confederate States of America. Davis is not here. Stephens is a member of the Congress....

Monday, February 18

This day, the inauguration of the President, Jefferson Davis, took place: he standing on the steps of the Capitol. I was selected by the Committee of arrangements to serve as Chaplain.... I rode in a coach drawn by six gray horses, in company with the President

and Vice President, and…our military escort.... The
ceremonies were prefaced by prayer, as follows:

"O Thou great Spirit! Maker and Lord of all
things! Who humblest thyself to behold the
things that are done on earth; and before whom
the splendor of human pageantry vanisheth
into nothing! By Thee Rulers bear sway: Thou
teachest senators wisdom. We own thy kind
providence, Thy fatherly care, in the peaceful
origin of the government of these "Confederate
States of America." We thank thee for the quiet
considerate unanimity which has prevailed
in our public councils; and for the hallowed
auspices under which the government of our
choice begins. Let thy special blessing rest on
the engagements and issues of this day. Thou
hast provided us a man to go in and out before
us, and to lead thy people. Oh vouchsafe thy
blessing, on this thy servant! Let his life and
health be precious in thy sight. Grant him a
sound mind in a sound body. Let all his acts
be done in thy fear, under thy guidance, with
a single eye to thy glory, and crown them all
with thy approbation and blessing! With the
like favors, bless the Congress of the "Confederate States"; and all who are, or may be,
charged by lawful authority with public cares
and labors. Put thy good spirit into our whole
people, that they may faithfully do all thy

fatherly pleasure. Let the administration of this government be the reign of truth and peace; let righteousness, which exalteth a nation, be the stability of our times, and keep us from Sin, which is a reproach to any people; establish Thou the work of our hands upon us; turn the counsel of our enemies into foolishness; and grant us assured and continual peace in all our borders; We ask all, through Jesus Christ Our Lord, Amen."[3]

Honorable Howell Cobb, President of Congress, administered the oath of office: the President laying his left hand on the table, and reverently holding up his right hand. At the close of the oath, the President *audibly repeated* the concluding words, "So help me, God!"

The day was pleasant and the pageant was very fine. I believe it was the largest crowd I ever saw together. May the blessing of God rest on this government of the Confederate States!

---

3. This appears to be Manly's prayer.

SELECTIONS FROM
Basil Manly, Jr.

B. Manly, March 1881.

Basil Manly, Jr.

14

Baptist psalmody

1. God with us, O glorious (oh, wondrous) name![1]
   Manifest in flesh he came.
   Hiding in a form like mine
   All his attributes divine.

2. Equal with the Father, still
   He obeys his Father's will,
   Lays his rightful glories by,
   Comes as man, for man to die.

3. While as a man on earth to dwell,
   As a (true) God, his power was felt;
   At his voice diseases fled,
   Opening graves restored their dead.

---

1. In Basil Manly, Sr., and B. Manly, Jr., eds., *The Baptist Psalmody: A Selection of Hymns for the Worship of God* (Charleston: Southern Baptist Publication Society, 1850), hymn 138. From Nathan Harold Platt, "The Hymnological Contributions of Basil Manly Jr. to the Congregational Song of Southern Baptists" (D.M.A. dissertation, Southern Baptist Theological Seminary, 2004), 236–237.

4. As a man, he groans and dies,
   Prisoned in the tomb he lies;
   Soon he rises from the grave —
   Man to die, but God to save.

———•••———

1. Holy, holy, holy, Lord,[2]
   God of hosts, in heaven adored,
   Earth with awe has heard thy name,
   Men thy majesty proclaim.

2. Just and true are all thy ways,
   Great thy works above our praise;
   Humbled in the dust, we own,
   Thou art holy, thou alone.

3. In thy sight the angel band
   Justly charged with folly stand;
   Holiest deeds of creatures lie
   Meritless before thine eye.

4. How shall sinners worship thee,
   God of spotless purity?
   To thy grace all hope we owe;
   Thine own righteousness bestow.

———•••———

2. In Manly and Manly, eds., *Baptist Psalmody*, hymn 21. From Platt, "Hymnological Contributions of Basil Manly Jr.," 237.

1. Jesus my Lord, I own thee God;[3]
   Earth sprang to being at thy nod;
   All things were made by thee, the Word,
   Who wast with God, as God adored.

2. Before the world's firm base was laid,
   Thy glorious Godhead was displayed;
   And after worlds have ceased to be,
   Thy praise shall fill eternity.

3. Thou, gracious Lord, my soul would own,
   The power to save is thine alone;
   O'er me assert thy sovereign will,
   And be my God, my Saviour still.

———••———

1. Lord, I deserve thy deepest wrath,[4]
   Ungrateful, faithless I have been;
   No terrors have my soul deterred,
   Nor goodness wooed me from my sin.

2. My heart is vile, my mind depraved,
   My flesh rebels against thy will;
   I am polluted in thy sight,
   Yet, Lord, have mercy on me still!

3. In Manly and Manly, eds., *Baptist Psalmody*, hymn 436. From Platt, "Hymnological Contributions of Basil Manly Jr.," 238.

4. In Manly and Manly, eds., *Baptist Psalmody*, hymn 445. From Platt, "Hymnological Contributions of Basil Manly Jr.," 238–239.

3. Without defence, to thee I look,
   To thee, the only Saviour, fly;
   Without a hope, without a friend,
   In deep distress to thee I cry.

4. Speak peace to me, my sins forgive,
   Dwell thou within my heart, O God,
   The guilt and power of sin remove,
   And fit me for thy blest abode.

⸻ ••• ⸻

1. There is a light which shines from heaven[5]
   On thee, but not alone for thee;
   Light of the world, for all 'tis given,
   And each may say 't was sent for me.

2. There is a fountain sweeter far
   Than aught earth's turbid springs can give;
   It makes the thirsting heart rejoice,
   The faint be strong, the dying live.

3. Drink of that fountain; rich it flows,
   Of life and joy a ceaseless spring;
   Drink deep; nor hide it for thyself,
   But all me to the fountain bring.

4. Wide let the healing water spread,
   Tell distant nations where 'tis found—

---

5. In Manly and Manly, eds., *Baptist Psalmody*, hymn 1023. From Platt, "Hymnological Contributions of Basil Manly Jr.," 239–240.

It comes from God, to him it leads,
Its murmur is the gospel's sound.

5. Let the light shine, the waters flow,
   The blessed news to all men take,
   That dying they may rise to life,
   And in the bliss of heaven awake.

John A. Broadus (1827–1895)

(Image used by permission of the Southern Baptist
Theological Seminary Archives)

15

Forming a new seminary

Letter from Basil Manly, Jr., to John A. Broadus[1]

Richmond, Virginia, May 14, 1858

As we are "fellow-partners," if not "in distress," at least in doubt and anxiety as to our duty, I do not know that I can more easily concentrate and make clear to myself the various considerations which bear upon the decision, than by writing to you. I find a pen helps me to think.

The first thing which strikes me is that a peculiar conjuncture of circumstances, not of our seeking or desire, has thrown the burden of this enterprise [to form a new seminary] on us.[2] It can hardly be wrong to call them providential circumstances. The idea has long been entertained, long labored for; the hope of fulfilling it has given

---

1. Basil Manly, Jr., to Broadus, in A. T. Robertson, *Life and Letters of John A. Broadus* (1901; repr., Harrisburg, Va.: Gano Books / Sprinkle Publications), 149–152.

2. This letter and the following one reveal the pathos over various concerns both Manly and Broadus had just prior to making their final decisions to leave their respective places of ministry and launch out into the waters of a new and overwhelming enterprise of the new seminary.

rise to every denominational college and has engrafted on most of them some special teaching looking toward theological instruction; never before has there seemed any opportunity at all—not to say so promising an opening—for accomplishing the result; though our acceptance does not indeed assure success, our declining, it seems necessary to confess, insures failure. Shall it fail? and shall the disappointment in this instance serve as a lasting discouragement, a decisive and unanswerable objection to all similar attempts? This is a question for you and me.

In fact it is narrower still. So far as I can see, the real decision rests with *you*.[3] If you decline, I think Poindexter will.[4] If he and you decline, I certainly shall. Then Winkler[5]

---

3. Broadus had a difficult time making the decision to leave his work at the Charlottesville (First) Baptist Church. For a fuller discussion of Broadus's reluctance to leave his church ministry, see Craig C. Christina, "Broadus and the Establishment of The Southern Baptist Theological Seminary," in *John A. Broadus: A Living Legacy*, ed. David S. Dockery and Roger D. Duke (Nashville: Broadman & Holman, 2008), 122–155.

4. This is a reference to Abram Maer Poindexter (1809–1872), a Baptist minister from Virginia. On Poindexter, see William Cathcart, ed., *Baptist Encyclopedia* (Philadelphia: Louis H. Everts, 1881), 923–924. When Manly was drawing up the Abstract of Principles, he consulted Poindexter, among others. See Cox, "Life and Work of Basil Manly, Jr.," 146–147. For a reference to one of Poindexter's sons, see below, page 212.

5. This reference is to Edwin T. Winkler (1823–1863), who at the time was serving as the pastor of the First Baptist Church, Charleston, where Manly's father had been pastor. He was active in the formation of the Southern Baptist Theological Seminary. For a study of his life and thought, see Tom Nettles, *The Baptists: Key People Involved in Forming a Baptist Identity* (Fear, Ross-shire: Christian Focus Publications, 2005), 2:323–361.

will feel unwilling to leave his church, even if he could otherwise be induced to go, and even [James] Boyce,[6] left alone, will feel himself compelled to look rather cheerlessly for new associates, men of more self-sacrifice (or I take that back—what I should have said is, men of more deep convictions of the comparative importance of such a seminary), or else he too must give up the ship, a grand *finale* indeed, after all that has been said and done....

I hear a great deal here that seems to me mere talk, or at any rate mere feeling, not entitled to rank as judgment or advice; the audacity of people is strongly censured who venture thus to *rob* Virginia, who entice away her strongest men, who expect to build up South Carolina at the expense of the other States, etc. Then there is more of objection than I had supposed possible among well-instructed men, to the whole idea of ministerial cultivation. An uneducated minister, it is said, has more sympathy with his people; instruction only lifts him up above them, puffs him up, etc. To this I say, jocosely, that if the students at the seminary never get more learning than their professors, they will never be hurt by the quantity of their learning, and more seriously, that the objection goes to the extent of doing away with all education, and that we must go back to the first principles. An educated man *can* speak plainly, in sympathy with his unlearned hearers, and be "all things to all men."[7] The uninstructed man cannot reach his cultivated hearers; he is debarred from

---

6. On James P. Boyce see above, page 26 n. 3.
7. 1 Corinthians 9:22.

one class, and that the more influential; the other has free access to both, etc....

Monday morning, May 17...Then some say there will be no students at Greenville [South Carolina], not more than twelve or fifteen at the outside; that to take the theological students away from Richmond College will be to render to that extent useless our expenditure there, and so too, of other States and colleges; that the endowment won't be collected to pay salaries, and that we will have to leave Greenville, starved out, in a year or two, both by the lack of money and the lack of anything to do; that a bird in the hand is worth two in the bush, etc.

Well, I have tried candidly and carefully to look at the subject all around; and I trust I have sincerely and humbly implored divine guidance. The present inclination of my judgment is, that I must go if the others go.... The question seems brought to our door, and laid at our feet, "So far as you are concerned, shall this seminary live, or disgracefully die?"

I have been trying to drink in the full richness of that text, "my mother's text." "Acknowledge the Lord in all thy ways, and he will direct thy paths."[8] God bless you and guide you, my brother.

---

8. Proverbs 3:6.

Letter from Basil Manly, Jr., to John A. Broadus [9]

Richmond, Virginia, May 18, 1858

As to the Seminary in Greenville, I think your declinature, under the circumstances, is the death blow to it. While I cannot in the smallest degree blame you for your decision, I may say that I regret it. I had made up my mind, if you accepted, that I would make an effort to induce Brother Poindexter's[10] acceptance, and if successful, I would accept. As it is, I think it doubtful, exceedingly so, whether he will undertake it. He and you declining, I think my duty is clear, so far as I can now see, i.e., not to go to Greenville. What shall I do, I know not. God, I trust, will guide me.

I do not know whether you can reconsider your determination. That is not for me to decide. There has been no opportunity, since I knew anything about the Baptists, when there was so fair an opportunity for a theological seminary as this. There will not probably be another for twenty-five years to come if this fails. As I now view the matter, it is already de facto a failure[11] — so soon as your decision and its results are known.... God bless you.

---

9. From Robertson, *Life and Letters of John A. Broadus*, 152–153.

10. On Poindexter, see above, page 140 n. 4.

11. Manly intimates here that if Broadus does not agree to take a position at the seminary, then the entire venture is a failure.

THE
SOUTHERN BAPTIST
THEOLOGICAL SEMINARY

16

Abstract of Principles[1]

Every professor of the institution shall be a member of a regular Baptist church; and all persons accepting professorships in this seminary shall be considered, by such acceptance, as engaging to teach in accordance with, and not contrary to, the Abstract of Principles hereinafter laid down, a departure from which principles on his part shall be considered grounds for his resignation or removal by the Trustees, to wit:

I. The Scriptures

The Scriptures of the Old and New Testaments were given by inspiration of God, and are the only sufficient, certain and authoritative rule of all saving knowledge, faith and obedience.

---

1. Cited in Cox, "Life and Work of Basil Manly, Jr.," 151. When the original charter of the Southern Baptist Theological Seminary was adopted in 1858, it contained this statement of principles, which continues as a part of the fundamental laws of the Seminary.

For an online version of Abstract of Principles, see http://www.sbts.edu/about/truth/abstract/.

For a discussion of this text, see above, pages 36–40.

II. God

There is but one God, the Maker, Preserver and Ruler of all things, having in and of Himself, all perfections, and being infinite in them all; and to Him all creatures owe the highest love, reverence and obedience.

III. The Trinity

God is revealed to us as Father, Son and Holy Spirit each with distinct personal attributes, but without division of nature, essence or being.

IV. Providence

God from eternity, decrees or permits all things that come to pass, and perpetually upholds, directs and governs all creatures and all events; yet so as not in any wise to be the author or approver of sin nor to destroy the free will and responsibility of intelligent creatures.

V. Election

Election is God's eternal choice of some persons unto everlasting life — not because of foreseen merit in them, but of His mere mercy in Christ — in consequence of which choice they are called, justified and glorified.

VI. The Fall of Man

God originally created Man in His own image, and free from sin; but, through the temptation of Satan, he transgressed the command of God, and fell from his original holiness and righteousness; whereby his posterity inherit a nature corrupt and wholly opposed to God and His law, are under condemnation, and as soon as they are capable of moral action, become actual transgressors.

VII. The Mediator

Jesus Christ, the only begotten Son of God, is the divinely appointed mediator between God and man. Having taken upon Himself human nature, yet without sin, He perfectly fulfilled the law; suffered and died upon the cross for the salvation of sinners. He was buried, and rose again the third day, and ascended to His Father, at whose right hand He ever liveth to make intercession for His people. He is the only Mediator, the Prophet, Priest and King of the Church, and Sovereign of the Universe.

VIII. Regeneration

Regeneration is a change of heart, wrought by the Holy Spirit, who quickeneth the dead in trespasses and sins enlightening their minds spiritually and savingly to understand the Word of God, and renewing their whole nature, so that they love and practice holiness. It is a work of God's free and special grace alone.

IX. Repentance

Repentance is an evangelical grace, wherein a person being by the Holy Spirit, made sensible of the manifold evil of his sin, humbleth himself for it, with godly sorrow, detestation of it, and self-abhorrence, with a purpose and endeavor to walk before God so as to please Him in all things.

X. Faith

Saving faith is the belief, on God's authority, of whatsoever is revealed in His Word concerning Christ; accepting and resting upon Him alone for justification and eternal life. It is wrought in the heart by the Holy Spirit, and is accompanied by all other saving graces, and leads to a life of holiness.

XI. Justification

Justification is God's gracious and full acquittal of sinners, who believe in Christ, from all sin, through the satisfaction that Christ has made; not for anything wrought in them or done by them; but on account of the obedience and satisfaction of Christ, they receiving and resting on Him and His righteousness by faith.

XII. Sanctification

Those who have been regenerated are also sanctified by God's word and Spirit dwelling in them. This sanctification is progressive through the supply of Divine strength, which all saints seek to obtain, pressing after a heavenly life in cordial obedience to all Christ's commands.

XIII. Perseverance of the Saints

Those whom God hath accepted in the Beloved, and sanctified by His Spirit, will never totally nor finally fall away from the state of grace, but shall certainly persevere to the end; and though they may fall through neglect and temptation, into sin, whereby they grieve the Spirit, impair their graces and comforts, bring reproach on the Church, and temporal judgments on themselves, yet they shall be renewed again unto repentance, and be kept by the power of God through faith unto salvation.

XIV. The Church

The Lord Jesus is the head of the Church, which is composed of all His true disciples, and in Him is invested supremely all power for its government. According to His commandment, Christians are to associate themselves into particular societies or churches; and to each of these churches He hath given needful authority for administering that order, discipline and worship which He hath appointed. The regular officers of a Church are Bishops or Elders, and Deacons.

XV. Baptism

Baptism is an ordinance of the Lord Jesus, obligatory upon every believer, wherein he is immersed in water in the name of the Father, and the Son, and of the Holy Spirit, as a sign of his fellowship with the death and resurrection of Christ, of remission of sins, and of giving himself up to God, to live and walk in newness of life. It is prerequisite to church fellowship, and to participation in the Lord's Supper.

XVI. The Lord's Supper

The Lord's Supper is an ordinance of Jesus Christ, to be administered with the elements of bread and wine, and to be observed by His churches till the end of the world. It is in no sense a sacrifice, but is designed to commemorate His death, to confirm the faith and other graces of

Christians, and to be a bond, pledge and renewal of their communion with Him, and of their church fellowship.

XVII. The Lord's Day

The Lord's Day is a Christian institution for regular observance, and should be employed in exercises of worship and spiritual devotion, both public and private, resting from worldly employments and amusements, works of necessity and mercy only excepted.

XVIII. Liberty of Conscience

God alone is Lord of the conscience; and He hath left it free from the doctrines and commandments of men, which are in anything contrary to His word, or not contained in it. Civil magistrates being ordained of God, subjection in all lawful things commanded by them ought to be yielded by us in the Lord, not only for wrath, but also for conscience sake.

XIX. The Resurrection

The bodies of men after death return to dust, but their spirits return immediately to God—the righteous to rest with Him; the wicked, to be reserved under darkness to the judgment. At the last day, the bodies of all the dead, both just and unjust, will be raised.

XX. The Judgment

God hath appointed a day, wherein He will judge the world by Jesus Christ, when every one shall receive according to his deeds; the wicked shall go into everlasting punishment; the righteous, into everlasting life.

17

"Soldiers of Christ, in truth arrayed"[1]

1. Soldiers of Christ, in truth arrayed,
   A world in ruins needs your aid;
   A world by sin destroyed and dead;
   A world for which the Saviour bled.

2. Forth to the realms of darkness go,
   Where, like a river's ceaseless flow,
   A tide of souls is drifting down,
   Blasted beneath th' Almighty's frown.

3. No human skill nor power can stay
   That flood upon its gloomy way;
   But God's own love devised the plan
   To save the ruined creature, man.

4. His gospel to the lost proclaim;
   Good news for all in Jesus' name;

---

1. From "Southern Baptist Theological Seminary: First Annual Commencement, May 28, 1860" (commencement program, 1860, four pages), p. 2. For an exposition of this hymn, see above, pages 45–58.

Let light upon the darkness break,
That sinners from their death may wake.

5. Morning and evening sow the seed;
God's grace the effort shall succeed;
Seed-times of tears have oft been found
With sheaves of joy and plenty crown'd.

6. We meet to part, but part to meet,
When earthly labors are complete,
To join in yet more blest employ,
In an eternal world of joy.

18

"Shall your brethren go to war, and shall ye sit here?"[1]

When the Israelites had conquered a part of the promised land, that part on the Eastern side of the Jordan, they remained many months encamped in the plains of Moab, whence they could look over to the richer and more populous region which was still to be subdued, and which constituted the choice and chief portion of their promised inheritance.

While there, the children of Reuben and Gad applied to have their portions assigned them at once, in this part of the country. The land was well adapted for pasture. These tribes were specially rich in flocks and herds, and they were desirous to secure so suitable a settlement.

Moses considered that this was the suggestion of insolence, avarice, or cowardice, or all three; and pro-

---

1. Basil Manly, Jr., *Halting on This Side of Jordan, or Shall Your Brethren Go to War, and Shall Ye Sit Here?* (Raleigh, N.C., ca.1861–1865). Manly is reflecting on Numbers 32:6 and its context. For a digital version, see http://docsouth.unc.edu/imls/manlyb/menu.html, the University of North Carolina at Chapel Hill digitization project, *Documenting the American South.*

ceeded accordingly to admonish them strictly. It was not strange that such suspicions should rise in his mind. There had been similar shrinking before from their destiny, and their duty. His whole experience had evinced the stubbornness and perversity of the people whom he had been called to lead. He appeals to them by the memory of the sins and the punishments of their fathers. Happy are we, if a stronger appeal can be made to us, by the memory of our fathers' righteousness and blessings. Sad is it, when the righteous depart, and a generation rises up worse than their fathers.

It was to be remembered that the other tribes had received no lot, had not yet conquered their part; and they might complain, if one after another of the tribes were settled down, while they had still to fight for theirs, a land unseen and untrodden as yet by them. Moreover it was a bad precedent. The land, it had been understood, was to be divided by lot; and if these might select and claim their share, so might others, so might all. And, worse than all, it looked like disregard of the main central region, the true Land of Promise, like distrust of the power of God, to give them the whole land, like a breach of the compact implied in their setting out together to conquer the whole land. And so Moses presses them with the inquiry — "Shall your brethren go to war, and shall ye sit here?" and with the fearful warning — "Be sure your sin will find you out."[2]

They protested that they had no intention to commit the sin he supposed. They did not wish to take up their

---

2. Numbers 32:6 and 23.

abode leaving the rest of the tribe with diminished forces, and discontented hearts to go on, in discouragement, to attempt the conquest of the remainder of the land. They desired only to locate their families and leave their herds with the younger people as sufficient garrison for the fortified towns; but the armed men were ready to go over with their brethren to the war and aid them in reconquering the land, in which their fathers had dwelt. The proposition in this form is accepted by Moses and their wish is gratified.

It is doubtful whether this was their original purpose, or whether they were really guilty of the design which Moses charged upon them. It is certain, however, that a similar sin is committed now, and the analogous errors of our own time may admit of profitable consideration.

A good deal has been said, sometimes in the language of indignant denunciation, sometimes in the more caustic phrases of bitter ridicule, of those prudent "keepers at home" in these times of general peril, who are ready to avail themselves of the flimsiest pretext for exemption, and to slink behind feigned diseases, or trades and professions long abandoned, to shield them from an honorable discharge of their duty to the country.[3] It is not my intention, nor is it necessary, that I address a word to this class. They are not in the army — where this tract will find its circulation.

There is another war, however, in which we are engaged with a deadlier foe than the Yankees — a war

_____
3. Manly refers to the Civil War.

which demands and deserves the concentration of every man's powers, and which must be prosecuted with unanimous zeal, and with patient endurance to the — not bitter, but— glorious end. And yet there are those who are ready, in this spiritual warfare, to halt on this side of Jordan, to leave to others the toils and the honors of these celestial victories, to sit still while their brethren go to war. I am afraid there are some of these in the army.

1. There are some who "discourage the heart" of their brethren.[4] Everything in war depends on keeping up the spirit of the army. Defeat by overwhelming forces is nothing. Good soldiers can rally and try it again. But if the spirit is broken, whether by treacheries, by hardships and abuse, by multiplied desertions, by discouraging speeches from generals or comrades, failure is almost inevitable. Now there are, among those who profess to be Christians, some croakers, who never sing except to a mournful tune, some icebergs that radiate nothing except chilliness. Their influence, so far as they have any, is of a benumbing, deadening, freezing kind. Like followers who hang about the baggage trains of advancing regiments, always watching for a ride, they are always ready to be helped, always expecting to be taken care of and comforted, but never dreaming that they might help or take care of anybody else. They have to be left behind, sitting still, or even worse, holding back whenever their brethren go forth to war. Now such people are accountable, not only for the

---

4. Numbers 32:7.

harm they have individually done and for the good they ought to have done, which they omitted, but also for the evil influence exerted on the others and the good in them which has been paralyzed. Are you one of these?

Do you sit still when the trumpet sounds? When you see anyone trying to advance the cause of Jesus, do you think he would be strengthened or discouraged by the course you take? Or does your manner and your conduct say to him, and to those whom he is trying to warn of their sin and danger, "It is a false alarm, and you had better do as I do, sit still"? It is very discouraging to those, who, with true zeal, are laboring to win souls, and especially to those unconverted persons who have begun to feel some concern about their souls, when they find entire indifference on the subject shown by those who profess to be Christians. These stationary Christians are the trees behind which sinners shelter themselves, and skirmish, alas, with painful success. Are you one of them?

2. There are some who attend to their own conveniences and personal comfort first, not only with a profound disregard how it may affect anyone else, but with entire forgetfulness of its effect on their own eternal interests. The land which these Reubenites and Gadites chose was goodly for situation, and suited exactly for their herds. But this haste to select and settle on their part looked like greater regard for their own interest than for the general good. So is there not now sometimes more anxiety for the advancement of a particular denomination, than for the true progress of the cause of Christ? Is there not some-

times a willingness to build up at another's expense, to hinder one promising enterprise lest the magnitude and importance of some other might be diminished?

Perhaps, in Reuben's case, there was something of pride in it. He was the first born of Israel, but had lost his birth-right. Several of the tribes, Judah and Ephraim especially, had risen above him in numbers, wealth and influence, so that he could not expect in an equitable division, the best lot: therefore to sow the shadow of a birthright where he had forfeited the substance, he catches at the first lot, though out of Canaan, and far off from the tabernacle. Now religion has prior claims on all men. It demands in every heart the first place, the best place; but most men are eager to seek first all other things, and then the Kingdom of God, and his righteousness. Now both classes of things need attention; but suppose we reverse this usual order, and adopt the one which Jesus enjoins. Then we shall obtain the righteousness of God, and all other needful things shall be added besides. The selfish, worldly choice is often, as in the case of Reuben and Gad, shown to have been least truly wise. First located indeed, they were but first displaced afterwards, first relapsing into idolatry, first carried into captivity, first passing into extinction. Severed gradually in interest and in sympathies, from those on the other side of the river, attempting a miserable neutrality, when enemies assailed the common cause, and buying inglorious and fatal peace instead of daring and winning in honorable warfare, their history remains a warning of what awaits those who hang back when common duty demands general sacrifices.

Now, that religion demands some sacrifices, some self denial, some energy, no one can deny. Its rewards cannot be obtained except at such a price; nor is this strange. Nothing else that is valuable is attainable without effort. Alas, there are many who are too indolent to be saved, too inert to receive a heavenly crown, who sit still when others are pressing on to the prize, who love their ease so well as to lose their souls.

3. There are those who stop short in Christian progress, as if all the work were accomplished. They have been just converted, perhaps, and conclude that now the important work is done. It is a mistake. It is just begun. They have only enlisted. They have yet to learn the use of their weapons, to acquire, by patient exercise, skill, rigor, endurance; and then, this is only preliminary to actual engagements and real triumphs.

Or possibly, they are Christians who have lost the warmth of their first love, and who have now begun to feel well satisfied with themselves just when there is greatest reason for self reproach and self condemnation. They are as good as they need to be, as good as they are expected to be, as good — yes, as good as they now want to be. Sad case! Their brethren are warring with all their might against the sins that still annoy, but Satan has lulled them into a delusive calm, a fatal slumber. They are sitting still, while their foundations are crumbling beneath them.

Incessant vigilance is the price of success in human warfare. It is even more so in the spiritual, as our enemies are more watchful, eager and powerful. There must be constant aggression on the army of Satan. Every birth adds one to the ranks of evil: the hosts of God are losing by every death, and can only be replenished by conversions, by winning over our opponents.

4. There are some who are always leaving their own work to be done by others. It is so in worldly matters; it is so in spiritual matters. Everyone has some work to do in this world. If not, he would not be left here, if he is already converted and fit for heaven. He would be taken thither at once. But the Master has appointed him, his time, his place, and his work too. There is a curious feeling among many that there is a great deal to be done in the Redeemer's cause, very important to be done, in fact absolutely indispensable, and a very firm conviction that somebody ought to do it, without the idea once occurring to them that they have a share in the responsibility. This necessary labor is to be done by certain nameless persons, of whom all they know is, that *they* are not of the number. Christians ought to do so and so. It would be a shame for the church to do without this, or to neglect that. And yet, if all Christians did exactly as much, in proportion to their ability, to promote these desirable ends, as they do, there would be nothing done.

No man can possibly do another man's work in religion. I do not mean merely that no man can do another's thinking, praying, believing for him; that no man can repent for another's sins, or exercise love and reverence to God in his place. But even those external acts, in which it seems more reasonable that the extra energy of one may supply the deficiencies occasioned by another's indolence, even those must be done by each one for himself.

Let us see how this is. Suppose there is a certain amount of visiting the sick, of personal effort with the unconverted, of other Christian labors, which devolves on a particular church, or on a number of Christians casually thrown together, as in an army. God knows how much it is, and he has portioned it out, so as to require of each one just as much as his due — no more — no less. And he has told us how much this is. He requires of each of us to serve and love him with all the heart, soul, mind, strength. No one can do more than this. Now, one man flinches from his duty, neglects it, overlooks it, and thinks to shift it on another's shoulders. That is impossible. Your neighbor cannot possibly undertake one jot or tittle of your work, because his hands are full — or ought to be — of his own. If you neglect it, it goes undone, necessarily undone — undone forever.

Every moment wasted, every opportunity lost of doing good, every favorable opening neglected, not only returns not to you, but offers itself to no other. It is gone. Others may come to be in like manner neglected and in like manner to pass away; but these come no more to you, or to any. Good men do, indeed, sometimes by neglecting their own proper work, attempt to supply the place left vacant by the folly or negligence of others, but they leave their own place vacant, in part and for a time at least, in so doing. It is a painful and lamentable thing to see faithful and true men almost overwhelmed with the cast-off and neglected burdens of other men, which they are trying to bear, because they find their own efforts to do good hampered by the omissions and deficiencies of their associates, and their way clogged up by the undone duties others have left behind them.

There is a great work to be done for the salvation of the men in these Southern armies, a work which for many of them must be done soon, or not at all, a work which will bear on all the interests of our widely extended country, into which ere long these picked men of every district will be returning to season all circles with their influence, and to bless every community with the example of their virtues, or curse the land with the contagion of their vices. It has been often said, and truly, that there never was an army like ours. No sweepings of our streets, no floating froth, nor sunken dregs of our population made it up; but our best, our noblest, well nigh our all, are there. And, if this be true, never was such a field for usefulness opened before mortal man.

To this work of evangelizing the army, every Christian in it is specially invited. Chaplains, colporteurs, missionaries, all may do their utmost, and yet there is room. Some are faithfully trying to do their duty. What are you doing? Are you — can you be sitting still? They owe the Lord no more than you. They owe the souls of men no more than you. Why should they engage in the work of the Lord, and you not? If it is regarded as toilsome and onerous, should they bear it all? If it pays back rich spiritual profit, and real happiness, ought they to enjoy it exclusively? If the land to be won is rich, fertile, glorious, will ye sit idly here, while they go and gain it?

What has been said so far, applies mainly to such as profess religion. Have the unconverted no interest here too? It is for your soul that many are striving and praying. Shall others be concerned for you, and you unconcerned for yourself? Shall they enter into the combat for your deliverance, while you stand coolly by, neutral, indifferent?

Will you be satisfied to take the land this side of Jordan, the fair but deceitful pleasures of this world, for your portion, and give up a hope and a home beyond the grave? Alas! How soon shall you be compelled to leave them! Be sure your sin will find you out, if not before, [and] you will lament your wretched choice when you are called to pass over Jordan, with no kind hand to divide the waves. Ere you are settled in your boasted possessions, ere your houses have become warmed by your presence, you may be summoned away to another house, that appointed for all living. Or you may see your mistake earlier. You may choose as Lot; the fair and fertile plains of Sodom, and live to see it desolate and blackened with the curse of God.[5] No possessions are secure enough, no wealth ample enough to give true happiness without the favor of God. And with that, one can have peace passing all understanding, no matter what his earthly lot.

"Seek first the kingdom of God and his righteousness, and all these things shall be added unto you."[6]

---

5. See Genesis 13:1–11; 19:1–28.

6. Matthew 6:33.

Seminary relocation committee on Lookout Mountain

19

Deserting the cause of Christ[1]

In the beginning of the war, a youth (whom we will call Charles R.) joined the Confederate army. He seemed fired with hearty zeal for the defense of our assailed rights. His parents were of Northern birth, but of Southern residence and professed decided adhesion to Southern views.

The first few moments of the war, however, brought their place of abode within the enemy's lines. Their son's company was stationed to guard an important point, where across the waters [of] Hampton Roads,[2] the United States flag was full in view, beneath which his father and family had taken refuge. Every day, as he gazed over the wavy expanse, he could see where they dwelt, not reconciled apparently to the Yankee yoke, even if they had not become its aiders and abettors. What influences prevailed over his boyish mind cannot be certainly known. But somehow the longing to join them, or the dislike of camp

1. Basil Manly, Jr., *The Young Deserter* (tract, ca.1861–1865).
2. Hampton Roads is the name of both a body of water and the areas of land that surround it in southeastern Virginia.

restraints, or the fickleness of a boy, triumphed over his oath of enlistment, his conviction of the righteousness of our cause, and his dread of the perils of desertion.

The opportunity was not long wanting, which ripened his scarcely formed desire into action. Numerous light boats were drawn up along the beach, with which the men were accustomed to sport, sometimes fishing, sometimes barely amusing themselves with a brief excursion. One evening, as the gold of sunset was mingling with the silver that crested the waves, Charles R. entered a boat and pushed off. He floated about carelessly with the ebb tide, as it seemed for a while, by degree getting further and further out, till from the distance and the darkening twilight, he might safely venture more decided movements. Perhaps even then he paused, debating whether to go or return, but the attractions ahead were too strong. Behind him were his sworn comrades in arms. Before him loomed the enemy's castle, with the associates of his early life. To them his heart cleaved. The doubt was over. With all the speed his eager and practiced hand could give, he urged his boat to Fortress Monroe.[3] He was a successful deserter.

I have known some to enlist under the banner of Jesus, who seemed all animated with noble zeal, whose promptitude and ardor outran the diffidence of slower minds, and gave them promise of abundant and extensive usefulness. They "seemed to run well"[4] and received a confidence and

---

3. Fortress Monroe is the largest stone fortress in the United States. See http://www.geocities.com/hrforts/Fort_Monroe/history.htm.

4. Galatians 5:7.

position in the church, which gave them power afterwards to bring reproach on the cause. They were not, perhaps, deceivers at first. They meant well, felt earnest, thought themselves sincere; but there was no steadfastness, no principle, no actual renewal about them. Their true attachments were elsewhere. Their chosen associations, their strongest ties, their deepest feelings bound them to the enemy. And so, after a struggle with the shame of fickleness, and with the dread of their soul's peril, and with the obligation of their vows and covenants — they departed. It was not all at once, perhaps; not by vigorous and determined movements at first. But they went. They left the Lord, they left his people, they left his ordinances, they left his ways, they cast his book aside, they put his laws behind their back, they cut themselves off from Him and His. In the outset, perhaps, it was apparently a simple yielding to the stress of an ebbing tide to the breathing of an off-shore wind; it was but an imperceptible movement, unsuspected by others, possibly not fully determined on by themselves; but the tendency was away from God and goodness, it was prevailingly toward evil. The temptation grew stronger as the distance and the darkness of the soul increased, and at last they struck out straight to join the enemy.

Are there any such deserters in this camp? Are there any, who are likely to become such? Are there any, who are even now conscious of temptation, which is seducing them from God? Are there any who have begun that half-sportive, half-serious parleying which may soon subject them altogether to its snares? Are there any, who are even now swaying back and forth on the deceitful waves that lie between the regions of purity and evil, half questioning with themselves whether to return or stay?

You have not gone far. Therefore, it is easy to stop now. You are not yet determined to yield and go. Therefore determine at once not to go. Your danger may seem slight. It is for that very reason more likely to delude and destroy you. Your error from the path of duty may appear plausible, may almost seem extenuated, or excused by the circumstances around you. Therefore, take the more heed lest you fall.[5] Oh stop! Think where you are going! Pray for grace to Him that is able to keep you from falling.[6]

But perhaps there are some who have passed beyond this doubtful stage of indecision. You are not resisting temptations, not struggling against backsliding; you are not merely meditating a desertion, and hesitating before you begin. You have passed the Rubicon.[7] You have made your choice. You are free from the restraint of religious profession, and have cast the fear of God behind you. Well, you are a successful deserter. You have gone forth from God's people because you were not of them. And what now?

The vows of God are upon you. You have broken them, but the shattered links still cling around your soul and cannot be shaken off. You have renounced His service. But that does not alter the fact that you once voluntarily enlisted.

---

5. 1 Corinthians 10:12.

6. Jude 24.

7. "You have passed the Rubicon" is an idiom meaning to go past the point of no return.

And so you stand, before God and angels and men, as a breaker of your promise, as a conscious violater of a solemn, deliberate covenant with your God. Is it not so?

Your influence is most decidedly felt against the cause of Christ, which once you professed to honor. You are not only ranked with the enemy, but you are so ranked by our own deliberate preference. And you have power to do more to religion, than those who never professed to be Christians. Your conduct seems to say to the world that you have tried religion, and found it to be a delusion. You may say, this is not your meaning; but such, alas, is the interpretation, which those who do not love God will put on your testimony. They will delight to point to you and say, "There is a man who was one of the saints, but has grown wiser." They boast of your impiety, will strengthen themselves on your weak compliances, will glory in your shame.[8] They will take a fiendish satisfaction in dragging you with them to deeper and more damning degradation, because you once tasted of the good word of God, and the powers of the world to come.[9] Your vices will be the theme of peculiar merriment, because your hands have handled the holy sacrament. Your blasphemies will be greeted with special glee, because your lips have joined in the songs of heavenly praise. And your case will be urged as the convincing argument which should deter the giddy from serious thought, the thoughtful from conviction, the

---

8. Philippians 3:19.
9. Hebrews 6:4–5.

convinced from faith in Christ, the trembling believer from public profession. You will be made the stumbling block for the blind to stumble over into hell!

Your case is one of fearful danger, as well as aggravated sin. "He that despised Moses' law died without mercy, under two or three witnesses: of how much sorer punishment, suppose ye, shall he be thought worthy, who hath trodden under foot the Son of God, and hath counted the blood of the covenant, wherewith he was sanctified, an unholy thing, and hath done despite unto the Spirit of grace?"[10] There is in your case peculiar, tremendous danger lest you will lose your soul — lest the same influences which have drawn you aside, should keep you away from God — lest your previous profession of piety may itself become one of the most serious barriers to your becoming willing even to listen attentively to God's word — lest your former experience may hinder you forever from striving to enter in at the straight gate[11] — may shut you up without effort here, without hope hereafter.

Your case is only not desperate. There is salvation even for such as you, with Him who "is able to save unto the uttermost."[12] There is pardon for Deserters who repent and return. Listen! "Though your sins be as scarlet, they shall be as white as snow; though they be red like crimson, they shall be as wool."[13] It is said that this word

---

10. Hebrews 10:29.
11. Matthew 7:13–14.
12. Hebrews 7:25.
13. Isaiah 1:18.

scarlet means double dyed. Come, then, ye double-dyed transgressors, who have broken both God's law, and your own promises — come and try how freely, fully, Jesus can forgive. "Him that cometh unto me, I will in no wise cast out."[14] "The blood of Jesus Christ his Son cleanseth us from all sin."[15]

---

14. John 6:37.
15. 1 John 1:7.

Seminary building in Greenville, South Carolina

(Image used by permission of the Southern Baptist
Theological Seminary Archives)

20

Testing a call to the ministry[1]

What are the qualifications requisite for a minister of the gospel?

It need scarcely be said that piety is essential. No amount of talent, no extent of education, no apparent brilliancy of fervor, should ever be allowed to gain admission into the ministry for one whose piety there is a reason to doubt, or who has not a more than ordinary active and consistent holiness. A Christless minister is as horribly out of place as a ghastly skeleton in the pulpit, bearing a torch in his hand.

Good intellect, some facility in acquiring knowledge, and some capacity to speak, are obviously indispensable. If a man has not these, in some degree, at the outset, it is not likely he will acquire them, either during the process of education, or in the work of the ministry. A man, who

---

1. From Basil Manly, Jr., *A Call to the Ministry. The Introductory Lecture before the Southern Baptist Theological Seminary, Greenville, S.C.* (Greenville, S.C.: G. E. Elford's Job Press, 1866), 8–13. An online version is available at the IX Marks Ministry web site: http://www.9marks.org/CC/article/0,,PTID314526%7CCHID598016%7CCIID2127106,00.html.

cannot preach at all, before he comes to the theological seminary, rarely learns how afterwards.

And then common sense is a very important quality, a practical tact, in which often God has been training some, whom he calls, comparatively late in life from the counter, or the lawyer's desk, and who need not, therefore, count their time lost....

Energy of character is an important prerequisite. The duties of the ministry are such that an indolent man will find abundant temptations and plausible excuses, while he will be not merely useless, but positively hurtful. A sluggish body can be driven to work, a sluggish mind rarely, a sluggish heart never. There is the force of character, a habit of persisting and succeeding, a power to influence and kindle others, a capacity to inspire confidence and general esteem, which, whatever name may be given to it, is essential to success.

In regard to these qualifications, the churches are usually better judges than the individual himself, and must exercise their judgment with prudence and fidelity, under a solemn sense of their accountability, and "lay not careless hands on heads that cannot teach and will not learn."

There is another qualification, however, on which the question mainly turns: it is an ardent and self-denying desire to labor for the good of souls. This is not a natural quality. It must be implanted by the Holy Spirit, and become an abiding, decided, and effective habit of the soul.

Now, whether the Holy Spirit has actually wrought this in the heart, thus signing, sanctioning, and sealing the call, is to be ascertained in the same way as other influences of the Holy Spirit; not by voices and visions, not by mere transitory impression, or confident, yet groundless, persuasion, but by positive moral changes produced in the habitual temper, character, and desires. We should seek for evidence of the Holy Spirit's work in calling to the ministry, as we seek for evidence of his work in the converting the soul. Neither is ordinarily manifested by a token, which admits of no doubt or hesitation, which is incapable of being either strengthened or weakened by subsequent developments; but usually by a number of particulars, which, when compared with the word of God, prove possession of the characteristics demanded.

We do not deny that the evidence may be instantaneous and overwhelming. It may be. Regeneration itself we suppose to be always instantaneous; the evidence of it to the individual himself may be, or it may not. Sometime it is as the flash of noonday radiance at midnight. At other times, it is as the gradual coming of the dawn, doubts being dispelled, and darkness gradually dispersed, as the morning mists flee, and shadows lessen, before the advancing sun. So in regard to a call to the ministry. There is a diversity of operation, but the same Spirit.

This steadfast and divinely implanted desire to labor for souls is substantially what is meant by "the internal call." It may be distinguished from the early zeal, which young converts usually have, and which "generally subsides into a calm principle of benevolent activity" in their own particular sphere.[2] In the man truly called, it grows,

---

2. Manly is here quoting from James D. Knowles, "What is a call to the ministry?" *Congregational Magazine* 11 (London, 1834): 145.

it increases. As he reflects on it, and prays about it, the great salvation becomes greater and nearer to him than when he first believed; the guilt and ruin of immortal souls weigh heavily upon him; he feels impelled to warn them to flee the wrath to come.

Sometimes the thought presses on one, so that he cannot rest. The strongest promptings of self-interest, the greatest timidity and natural reserve, the most violent opposition of irreligious relatives and influential friends, and even the most serious peril, prove insufficient to check this holy ardor. The man is made to feel that for him all other avocations are trifling, all worldly employ-ments unattractive. "Woe is unto me," he cries, "if I preach not the gospel!"[3] Jails, and fetters, and the stake, have no terrors for him comparable with the guilt of disobeying Jesus, and the frown of his redeemer....

Sometimes, on the other hand, there is a more calm and gradual growth of a conviction of duty, drawn by delight rather that driven by dread. He loves to think of Jesus, and so he loves to talk of Jesus; and with much dis-trust of himself, perhaps, he finds an increasing desire to be wholly absorbed and occupied in such things. A calm and deliberate comparison of various courses of life shows him that the ministry offers arduous labor, with little worldly advantage or honor; heavy responsibility, painful to a sensitive nature; and a life-long toil, with no remis-sion till Jesus calls him to rest. But though consciously weak, he can simply rely on divine direction to guide,

---

3. 1 Corinthians 9:16.

and divine strength to uphold, and in view of the dying world and the bleeding cross and the burning throne, he can freely consecrate himself to be "Jesus Christ's man," to go where he bids, to utter what he teaches, to endure what he pleases to appoint, and thank God if he may be counted worthy to suffer for his name.

Now we need numbers in the ministry. The plenteous, perishing harvest wails out a despairing cry for more laborers. But we need purity more than numbers; we need intelligence more than numbers; we need zeal more than we need numbers. Above all, we need consecrated men, men who have stood beneath the cross, till their very souls are dyed with Jesus' blood, and a love like his for perishing millions has been kindled within them. We long for such men, but for such only, as are willing to "endure hardness as a good soldiers of Jesus Christ."[4]

If I address any young brother, whose mind may have been directed to this subject, allow me to present some practical inquiries, which may help you to come to a decision.

Do you habitually entertain and cherish the conviction that you are not your own; but, as dead with Christ, are bound to live not unto yourself, but unto him who died for you, and rose again?

Do you feel willing to serve him in whatsoever employment you can most glorify his name?

Do you watch for opportunities of doing good, and

---

4. 2 Timothy 2:3.

avail yourselves of those that offer, in the Sunday school, in the prayer meeting, and by the wayside?

Do you sincerely desire to make it the business of your life to labor for souls? Is the desire habitual, disinterested, and prompted by love to Jesus, and compassion for the impenitent?

Do you find that other employments seem comparatively uninviting, and this delightful, apart from any considerations of worldly ease or emolument?

Does your impression of duty with regard to the ministry grow stronger, at such times when you are most favored with nearness to God, and when you most distinctly realize eternal things?

Is your willingness to engage in such service connected with a clear and cordial renunciation of self-seeking, and a simple reliance on him whose grace is promised to be sufficient?

Is it joined with a humble estimate of your own powers, and with a willingness to use all necessary and suitable means for the improvement of those powers?

Is it a desire for this work, not as a temporary resort, as a refuge for indolence, or an avenue to fame, but as a lifetime labor, in prosperity or adversity, in evil report and in good report, that God may be honored and sinners saved?

21

"Come all who feel your sins a load"[1]

1. Come all who feel your sins a load,
   Pour complaints before your God;
   He is the Sinner's Friend indeed,
   He will not break the bruised reed.

2. A meek and lowly Saviour see,
   His love is vast, his grace is free;

---

1. From Platt, "Hymnological Contributions of Basil Manly Jr.,"
240. The hymn is to be found in Basil Manly, Jr., "Come all who feel
your sins a load," in his letter to Smith & McDougal, August 3, 1871,
Basil Manly Papers, vol. 5, James P. Boyce Centennial Library Archives,
Southern Baptist Theological Seminary, Louisville, Ky. These papers
will henceforth be cited as Basil Manly Papers with the respective volume and page number.

Smith & McDougal was a firm involved in the publication of *The
Baptist Praise Book: For Congregational Singing*, eds. Richard Fuller, E. M.
Levy, S. D. Phelps, H. C. Fish, Thomas Armitage, E. T. Winkler, W.
W. Everts, George C. Lorimer, and Basil Manly, Jr. (New York: A. S.
Barnes, 1871). Manly submitted this hymn to the hymnal committee as
a substitute for one he regarded as quite inadequate. In his words, "If
you can find nothing better to substitute for it, here is one which you
are at liberty to use if you wish." The committee did not use it. For this
letter, see also Paul Richardson, "Basil Manly, Jr.: Southern Baptist Pioneer in Hymnody," *Baptist History and Heritage*, 27 (April 1992): 26.

   To him your guilt and burden take,
   The bruised reed he will not break.

3. Wounded for love of us was he,
   And bruised for our iniquity;
   To heal our souls, behold him bleed!
   He will not break the bruised reed.

4. Come, weak and wounded, sick and sore.
   His strength receive, his grace adore;
   His promise firm can never shake,
   The bruised reed he'll never break.

22

Loving one's brethren

Letter to James P. Boyce[1]

September 11, 1871

Dear Bro.—

As to those vols. of Augustine, do me the favour to keep them as some token of our firm & unwavering friendship. I admired you for your work before I knew you intimately. And every day's acquaintance has only added to my esteem. If I do not tell you goodbye—you know it is not for any lack of affection. I trust we shall often meet in the future, & cooperate in the great work to which our lives have been devoted.

---

1. Basil Manly Papers, 5:252. This letter was written after Manly's decision to leave the seminary to take up the presidency of Georgetown College.

James P. Boyce (1827–1888)

23

Advice to a son in the ministry[1]

As I look back upon it [my life] it seems to me a great catalogue of short-comings. Much that I had planned, I have never attempted — much that I attempted has only partially succeeded. With dying Grotius, I feel much like exclaiming — "*Eheu, vitam perdidi laborious, nihil agenda*" ["I have spent my life laboriously doing nothing"].[2] As far as I can, I would like to guard you against my mistakes.

One of my besetting sins has been *procrastination*. This has not been purely a result of indolence, but often of indecision, and like many other faults, it has connected itself with a virtue, or at least assumed its semblance, i.e., the prudence which does nothing rashly, and decides nothing before time. Hence, often while hesitating, new information has come to me, which turned the scale of decision, and without which I might have decided wrongly. But on the other hand, sometimes while hesitating the golden moment for action has passed, and I have found myself

---

1. Basil Manly, Jr., to George Manly, September 28, 1878, Basil Manly Papers, 10:296–299. This letter is cited by Cox, "Life and Work of Basil Manly, Jr.," 275–277.

2. The Dutch jurist Hugo Grotius (1583–1645).

like the dilatory rustic, who is just too late for the train, gazing at the departing opportunity, open mouthed and astonished.

I have decided to fix for myself the rule always to do *the day's work in a day*; and when my work is of a sort that it can be measured off, and ascertained to be done, I can observe the rule pretty well. But much of my work is of a sort which knows no limit or completion.... The right apportionment of time, when either one of half a dozen things that claim one's attention is sufficient to absorb it all—is often a problem of no small difficulty.

This suggests another evil, which has led me astray often. It is that of so *multiplying the objects of my pursuit*, as not to have adequate concentration and unity of aim to attain the greatest success. I have labored at *many* things, rather than *much* at any of them. From a sort of general facility at doing almost anything that came up, and partly from a disposition to be obliging, this habit has gained too much dominion over me. Yet, I doubt it not, this versatility of talent and readiness to turn my hand to anything that came up, has been one of the elements of which usefulness I have achieved. While other professors neglected or refused I looked after what nobody else could be got to do...and thus I have been all my life a stopper of gaps, a bearer of cast off or neglected burdens of other men, uncomplainingly useful in the tasks that were unconspicuous, or even mere drudgery, but absolutely necessary. I think, however, that I might have accomplished more, on the whole, if I had been a man of one work, of one idea, if I had selected my mode of labor wisely, and then stuck to it. I have been preacher, teacher, editor, agent, financier, lawyer, farmer, doctor—all by turns as occasion seemed to demand, and sometimes several of them at once.

In my reading I was too *omnivorous*. I claimed and sought to possess all the varied fields of literature for my own. I do not mean that I could excel in all; but I sought to know something of it all. I separated myself and sought to "intermeddle with all knowledge."[3] While this gave me rather a wider range of information than is usually attained, it prevented me from the thoroughness and completeness in any one branch which I might perhaps have acquired. For example, I believe I taught, at one time or another, almost every branch at the Theological Seminary during some part of my connection with it, except Church Government, and I presume I could have done as well as some of the others, if it had been desirable for me to try it. Yet there was no branch in which I attained a marked and indisputable excellence. I was fair in all, superior in none. So, in College and in the Female Institute[4] I have taught some of almost every department in the whole curriculum, and possibly have done it not discreditably, but I have been brilliantly or conspicuously successful in none. The things I know nothing about are few; there is nothing I know all about.

I feel that one of my great weaknesses and the source not only of discomfort but of failure has been the *lack of prayer*. Prayer has not been with me a mockery, a mere

---

3. See Proverbs 18:1.

4. Georgetown College, Kentucky, and Richmond Female Institute, Virginia. See above, pages 29–31.

form. But it has been grievously defective both in amount and in earnestness. I have not prayed enough. I have not studied the common English Bible enough. While God has been waiting to talk with me, through the lips of David, Isaiah, Paul — I have been listening to some trifling talker, absorbed in some trifling newspaper, or interested in some exciting word. If I had my life to go over again, I would give more time to daily secret prayer and to the reading of the English Scriptures, in the common and revised versions — using the marginal references to compare parallel passages and thus to interpret Scripture by Scripture.

Most of all, dear George, *watch your heart* — not with a brooding, morose, remorseful disgust, that discourages rather than corrects or guards — but with a[n] honest cheerful desire to avoid the occasions of evils which have ensnared you, and to fight manfully against the impulses, which you have found to draw you downward and away from God.

To me a theological course was not a temptation but a spiritual experience — especially after I went to Princeton. I think I grew in grace by it. God grant it may be so with you.

24

Divine inspiration[1]

I have felt some hesitation in replying to yours [letter] of December 22, [1881,] because as Professors in the Southern Baptist Theological Seminary, we have always been averse to making statements or decisions, as if possessing authority other than pertaining to any reputable minister of the Gospel. Yet I feel that courtesy to you demands of me personally a frank reply as to my own teachings.

The only authoritative document of our seminary on the subject of doctrine is our "Fundamental Articles," of which the first is: "The Scriptures of the Old and New Testament were given by inspiration of God, and are the

---

1. Basil Manly, Jr., to Norman Fox, January 4, 1882, Basil Manly Papers, vol. 12, part 1, pp. 425–426. Cited in Cox, "Life and Work of Basil Manly, Jr.," 320–321. Three years earlier Manly had stated: "Every school and department of the seminary is mainly valuable as it promotes the elucidation of the Word of God, and the practical application of its teachings. Nor do we fear being charged with bibliolatry in giving the Bible the central, dominant place in our system and in our affections. From the doubt or denial of God's book, the road is short to doubt or denial of God;—and after that comes *the abyss*, where all knowledge is not only lost but scoffed at, except that which the brute might enjoy as well" ("Why and How to Study the Bible," cited in George, introduction to *Bible Doctrine of Inspiration*, 10).

William Williams (1821–1877)

(Image used by permission of the Southern Baptist
Theological Seminary Archives.)

only sufficient, certain and authoritative rule of all saving knowledge, faith, and obedience."[2]

This language must be understood in accordance with the well known convictions and views of the founders of the Seminary, and of the Baptist denomination generally. While I am accustomed to insist on no *theory* of the manner in which inspiration was effected, I hold and teach the fact, that the Scriptures are so inspired as to possess infallibility and divine authority, and where fairly interpreted, to be an adequate guide in all matters of saving knowledge and of practice. This is what I understand by the expressions, "the *only sufficient, certain* and *authoritative* rule," etc. In brief, then, the points are the infallibility, the divine authority and the sufficiency of the Scriptures as the Word of God.

The subject of inspiration falls within the range of more than one of our professors, e.g., in Biblical Introduction, which I am teaching this year, and in Systematic Theology, which belongs to Dr. Boyce. Of course, however, it comes up incidentally in all departments, and I have no reason to believe there is any departure from the substance of the above teachings, while each Professor may adopt his own forms of expression.

---

2. See above, page 145.

A. H. Newman (1852–1933)

(Portrait used by permission of McMaster Divinity College,
McMaster University, Hamilton, Ontario)

25

Christian hospitality

Letter to A. H. Newman[1]

August 4, [188]5

Dear Bro.

I am pained to see in the morning papers of today & yesterday accounts of a serious fire, which has visited your beautiful city. I had so much pleasure in the cordial reception which I met with there, that I feel as if I was endowed with a sort of partial Citizenship, & had a kind of personal participation in its affairs & interests. I trust none of our personal friends were sharers in the losses.

I have been talking over our plans for building with

---

1. Basil Manly Papers, 15:868. A. H. Newman (1852–1933) was among the most distinguished church historians of this era. He was born in the Edgefield district, South Carolina, where Manly's father once served as a pastor. He was a graduate of Mercer University and Rochester Theological Seminary, New York, and spent 1875–1876 studying at Southern Baptist Theological Seminary when it was still in Greenville, South Carolina. Newman was one of the founding faculty of Toronto Baptist College in 1881, where he taught until 1901, when he went to Texas to teach at Southwestern Baptist Theological Seminary. For his life, see Frederick Eby, *Newman the Church Historian* (Nashville: Broadman Press, 1946).

the other Professors. The practical difficulty before us
[is]…where to get the money. We shall have to get it
in small sums from many hands. We have no one like-
minded with your noble Mr. McMaster.[2] God bless &
preserve him.

Please remember me very cordially to Mr. McMaster &
to Dr. Castle,[3] whose genial, kindly greetings remain with
me as a pleasing memory of Toronto. Most of all I prize the
cordiality & frank hospitality with which your good wife
made me feel at home at once. She took the "stranger" feel-

---

2. William McMaster (1811–1887) was an Irish immigrant from
Ulster who arrived in Toronto in 1833 and soon became a partner in,
and then sole proprietor of, a dry goods firm. Concentrating his energies on wholesaling, he became one of the wealthiest men in Toronto
and by the 1850s had entered into banking. He helped found the Cana-
dian Bank of Commerce in 1867, and as its first president he built it
into the leading bank in Ontario. A member of Jarvis Street Baptist
Church in Toronto, he provided the more than $100,000 to make pos-
sible the erection of the substantial Gothic church building that would
become the premier Baptist Church in Canada in the last quarter of
the nineteenth century.

McMaster was also instrumental in setting up Toronto Baptist
College on Bloor Street, Toronto. He gave an initial $100,000 to the
school's establishment and pledged an additional sum of $14,500 annu-
ally. Construction was finished in the summer of 1881, and classes
began that fall.

3. John H. Castle (1830–1890), an American, was pastor of Jarvis
Street Baptist Church, Toronto, where McMaster was a member. On
Castle, see B. D. Thomas, "Pulpit and Platform. 'A Servant of His Age'"
(sermon, Jarvis Street Baptist Church, Toronto, June 22, 1890), included
in B. D. Thomas, "My Pastorate in Toronto" (scrapbook of newspaper
clippings, McMaster Divinity College Archives, McMaster University,
Hamilton, Ontario). This memorial sermon for Castle, based on Acts
13:30, includes a biographical sketch of Castle at the end.

William McMaster (1811–1887)

ing out of my heart immediately, & made me feel as if I had known you all intimately for a score of years.[4]

My wife and children join me in kindest greetings to you & yours, & we hope to see you at our house some day.

Yours fraternally,

          — B. Manly

---

4. In a later letter, Manly told Newman that he felt Newman and his wife Mary were "almost *like kinfolks*" (Basil Manly, Jr., to A. H. Newman, April 23, [1888,] Basil Manly Papers, 19:315–316).

26

Responding to the "New Theology"

Letter to Matthew T. Yates[1]

It appears to me that the Pantheism of England and Germany is very little else than a re-vamped heathenism, scarcely more rational or elevating than that which Brahmins or Fire worshippers, or Egyptians had. They sometimes dress up their doctrines in a sentimental style, and bedeck the idol they have invented with a few Christian phrases—but the Christ they allow is one stripped of his Deity and authority, and the heaven they promise is one all open to the tread of the godless and profane—where culture counts instead of charity—and poetry serves for piety—and grace of person or movement or expression is accepted as a substitute for divine grace in the heart.[2]

---

1. Letter to Matthew T. Yates, March 6, 1884, Basil Manly Papers, vol. 21. Cited in Cox, "Life and Work of Basil Manly, Jr.," 337. Manly correctly describes German liberalism as it emerged in the nineteenth century.

2. Manly's conservative theological position is revealed in a number of texts written during the 1880s. For instance, when the Baptist theologian J. R. Graves (1820–1893) raised the question about the state

of believers after death and before the general resurrection, Manly said to him that he had "nothing new or startling to present, but only the old fashioned doctrine of our fathers" (Basil Manly, Jr., to J. R. Graves, June 30, 1882, Basil Manly Papers, vol. 12, part 1, p. 586). And in 1886, Manly expressed his delight at hearing of a correspondent's "adherence…to the grand doctrines of the old theology" (Basil Manly, Jr., to S. A. Smith, June 30, [188]6, Basil Manly Papers, 13:390–391).

27

The deficiencies of an uninspired Bible[1]

The difference between an inspired and uninspired Bible is of a momentous character. It is closely connected with the question whether we are following God or men, whether our religion is of divine or of human origin. An uninspired Bible, whatever its excellences might be, would have three serious defects.

First, it would furnish no infallible standard of truth. It would leave us liable to all the mistakes incident to failure of the writers, to errors in judgment, or their defective expressions of correct thought. It would be no principle of accurate discrimination between the true and the false, the divine and the human.

Second, it would present no authoritative rule for obedience and no ground for confident and everlasting hope. It would contain advice instead of commands, suggestions instead of instructions, surmises of good men (perhaps not even of good men) instead of promises of a faithful God. It

1. From Basil Manly, Jr., *Bible Doctrine of Inspiration*, 22–23.

would give no firm ground on which to base our convictions, to build our hopes or to order our life.

Third, it would offer no suitable means for testing
and cultivating the docile spirit, for drawing man's soul
trustfully and lovingly upward to its heavenly Father. It
would minister to the pride of reason, instead of to the
culture of faith. It would generate perplexity instead of
repose, conflict instead of submission, resistance instead
of reverence.

28

Inspiration and illumination[1]

It is important...to distinguish both revelation and inspiration from spiritual illumination, such as is common and necessary to all Christians. This last may be defined as that influence of the Holy Spirit under which all the children of God receive, discern, and feed upon the truth communicated to them. This is distinct from revelation and inspiration in several ways:

    a.   It is promised to all believers, and therefore is what every Christian may expect and pray for.

    b.   It is dependent on conditions, which may or may not be fulfilled by the individual.

    c.   It admits of degrees, increasing or diminishing in the same person, and varying greatly as it is actually found in different persons.

    d.   It is closely connected with personal character.

    e.   It conduces to and secures salvation.

None of these points is true with respect to revelation or inspiration.

---

1. Manly, Jr., *Bible Doctrine of Inspiration*, 38–40.

Spiritual illumination is confounded with inspiration by two large important classes:

1.   On the one hand, by the Roman Catholics, and
2.   On the other hand by the rationalists generally.

The former do it for the purpose of maintaining that the church, not only of primitive but of modern times, has an inspiration equal to that which gave the Bible. While theoretically claiming for the Spirit, which is alleged to be residing in the church, equal authority with the Bible, practically they exalt it to superiority over the Bible. They adroitly add the further unfounded assumption that *they* are this infallible church.

The latter class, claiming more or less to be the devotees of reason, confound this common influence of the Spirit with the extraordinary operations of revelation and inspiration. They do this in such a way as to attribute to the apostles and to the inspired record all the variability, uncertainty, and deficiency which are readily discovered in good men everywhere, acting under the usual leadings of the Holy Spirit in common life.

…That inspiration does not necessarily imply spiritual illumination in the sense explained, or insure the possession of saving grace, may be seen in the familiar instances of the prophet Balaam, or King Saul, or the high priest Caiaphas, who all spoke under divine influence, but, so far as we can judge, evidently without renewed hearts.

On the other hand, that spiritual illumination does not imply inspiration is apparent in the consciousness of every truly regenerated person today. It is a transparent fallacy to allege that, because the Spirit that works these two things is the same, therefore the operations are the same. We cannot assume that the Spirit can only act in one way on the children of God in different ages and circumstances....

The distinction we have indicated between revelation, inspiration, and illumination is not only obvious in the nature of the case, and required by the instances given, in which one of these influences is found without the other, but seems also suggested by the express language of the apostle Paul in 1 Corinthians 2:10–14.

He speaks first (verse 10) of the things naturally unknown which God has *revealed* through the Spirit.

Secondly, he speaks of the "Spirit which is of God" (verse 12) being received that under its illumination "we might *know* [appreciate or accept] the things that are freely given to us by God," and without which "the natural man *receiveth* not the things of the Spirit of God" (verse 14).

Thirdly (verse 13), he speaks of the power by which *they uttered* the things that had been revealed to them, "which things also we speak, not in words which man's wisdom teacheth, but which the Spirit teacheth."

Thus, what we have termed revelation, spiritual illumination, and inspiration, are each presented by the apostle in their proper relations and for their appropriate uses.

New York Hall, first building constructed by Seminary
in Louisville, Kentucky

29

"Our Brother in Black"[1]

The history of the Black Man in America is one of the most striking chapters in the providential dealings of God with this country. He is a factor that enters, sometimes most perplexingly, into every problem, social, financial, religious or political that agitates the public mind.

It is of no use for anyone to say, "We dislike him, we

---

1. Basil Manly, Jr., "Our Brother in Black," *Seminary Magazine*, vol. 2, no. 5 (May 1889): 137–139. The Southern Methodist Atticus G. Haygood (1839–1896) used this very title in a book written eight or so years earlier: *Our Brother in Black: His Freedom and His Future* (New York: Phillips & Hunt; Cincinnati: Walden & Stowe, 1881).

In A. James Fuller's biography of Basil Manly, Sr., Fuller included "Our Brother in Black" among Basil Manly, Sr.'s writings (*Chaplain to the Confederacy: Basil Manly and Baptist Life in the Old South* [Baton Rouge: Louisiana State University Press, 2000], 310–311), because the original handwritten version is among the elder Manly's papers in the South Carolina Historical Collection, James Buchanan Duke Library, Furman University, Greenville, South Carolina. But Fuller recently rethought his view and decided that "Our Brother in Black" "was indeed Jr.'s piece. Sr.'s handwriting became so different after his stroke that it was hard to tell who was actually writing what.... My sense is that if Jr. published it, the piece was his" (Fuller, e-mail to Michael A. G. Haykin, March 13, 2009).

will have nothing to do with him." He has to do with us, whether we will or not.

"But," says someone, "he ought not to be here, he ought never to have been brought here, he ought to be driven away, or coaxed, colonized, abolished." This novel kind of abolition is impracticable, and it is unwise and sinful to urge it even if it were possible. He is here, and he is going to stay. What are you going to do about it?

"But we don't care," says another, "what is done is done with him; we are going to mind our own business, and don't intend to care what becomes of him." It is part of your business to see what becomes of him. I am not ascribing exaggerated importance to the negro when I say that he cannot be ignored or neglected without harm to our land, that no class in it, however humble, can be injured or despised without affecting the welfare of all. The highest and lowest, the ignorant and the cultured, the laborer and the capitalist, the man of muscle and the man of mind are so blended and unified in our civil system, that their real interests are identical, and that each has share and sympathy in the prosperity of all.

The only way then to deal with the black man whom

Further proof of its being the work of the younger Manly is that it was first published in *The Seminary Magazine* after the father's death and with no indication that it was written by the elder Manly. Anyone reading the magazine would assume it was by Basil Manly, Jr. In fact, after Basil Manly, Sr., died and the son moved to Louisville, the son dropped the use of Jr. when signing his name ("Memoranda as to Basil Manly," October 19, 1880, Basil Manly Papers, vol. 12, part 1, pages 113–115).

we find in America — is to *give him his rights*, cordially, frankly, fully.

The freedman is a man, neither more or less. And it is not so much as a freedman that we are concerned about him. It is rather as a freeman. Whatever he was, this thing is certain: he is now a freeman, by the highest organic law of government, by the constitution of the United States, by the separate action of the respective states. His past condition of servitude is not unimportant as affecting his present state and our present responsibilities. But the momentous question is not what he was, but what he is, and especially what he is going to be. And with that question we have something to do.

He is not a babe to be fondled and petted. He is not a brute to be trampled and despised. He is not a fiend or a savage to be shunned and dreaded, nor an angel to be admired and flattered. He is simply a man with the capabilities and duties of any other man, so far as he is competent to discharge them, liable to the same temptations and frailties, heir of the same immortality, and redeemed by the same precious blood.

In the confusion and heat of the popular mind, and with so many clashing interests, the prejudices which have been growing for many generations, the partisan statements colored conspicuously, or consciously to serve a purpose, it is not easy to say in all respects what is right. Oh how hard it is to know, and how harder still to do just what is right!

Sometimes those who are aiming at the same thing misapprehend and bitterly antagonize each other's plans, and so inadvertently cripple their best allies. The artillerist in the smoke and disorder of battle may sweep away the ranks of his friends. We cannot afford to act unwisely or inefficiently any more than we can afford not to act at all.

Hence I am always glad when good men are honestly consulting and enquiring into this important matter: when the question is — not how much can be got out of the colored man as a worker, nor how much use can be made of him as a voter — but how much can be put into him as a man, how much can be done for him as an immortal.

What does he need?

First and foremost, he needs to be fairly treated. To have the truth told about him, the whole truth if practicable, but at all events nothing but the truth: to have fair opportunity for labor, and to get honest pay for it; to have a chance to become educated, and to develop whatever there is in him, in good and noble directions; in short to have a fair field.

I shall not draw any terrible pictures of their deplorable state, with a good deal of red in the brush, for two reasons — first, they would not be true; and second, there is no need. There is enough to rouse any thoughtful man to action in the fact that here in our midst is to be found a nation within a nation, twice as great in number today as the whole American people were one hundred years ago when our independence was achieved. They are said to number now not less than seven millions and there were scarcely more than three millions of inhabitants in the thirteen original colonies.

What has been done to help? And what has been the

success of the efforts made? Without going into details it is sufficient to say — enough for encouragement, not enough for inaction. And in the emergency we welcome cordially the liberal aid of our Northern brethren, who have done, especially in the important matter of educational institutions, a work which in our crippled condition it would have been impossible for the South to have undertaken, or to carry through.

Let us each do all we can in this great enterprise, and commit our work to the kind care of Him who commended a humble act of loving devotion, and consigned it to everlasting remembrance, because "she had done what she could" (Mark 14:8).

Francis Wayland (1796–1865)

30

Firm faith[1]

Faith…is often grievously misunderstood.

1. It is supposed to be identical with a blind credulity, to be born of passion or prejudice or ignorance, to be antagonistic to reason. This is an utter misconception. Belief without evidence is not faith; it is credulity. Belief on religious or spiritual subjects without just evidence is superstition. Belief on legitimate and sufficient evidence is faith. And the only way to attain a satisfactory and permanent faith is to have it grounded on good evidence.

> Experience will batter down the walls that are built only by prejudice. A change in the wind or a fall of the barometer will be enough to ruin the edifices that are constructed only of emotion. The man who thinks he must be right just because he "feels so good" may lose his convictions by an attack of dyspepsia or a blast of the east wind. A

1. From Basil Manly, Jr., "Free Research and Firm Faith," *Christian Index* (October 15, 1891): 2–3. This was the 1891 commencement address given by Manly at the Newton Theological Institution, Newton Center, Massachusetts.

ray of sunshine may scatter many mists, and dis-
perse a whole army of imagined difficulties, the
children of darkness. Faith, it is true, gives us
knowledge of things unseen; but it is on the evidence of one who has seen.

2. Another grievous misconception of faith is that which
limits it chiefly to a persuasion concerning our own
selves. A firm faith is, in the eyes of some, mainly a firm
conviction of one's own salvation, a conviction often
grounded on very shallow and superficial, or even on mistaken, evidence. Direct their minds to the fact that faith
should be upward-looking, not inward-looking; that, if
it is to be the anchor of the soul, it should take hold of
"that which is within the veil";[2] that the anchor should
not be snugly resting on the side of our own vessel, or
floating in fathomless depths and dragged withersoever
we ourselves are driven; that faith must be in Christ, not
in themselves — they are amazed at such novel ideas and
exclaim that we have taken away their hope. Better lose
such a groundless hope than be lost because of indulging
it. Faith is that which saves. It cannot, then, be simply
a strong persuasion that we are saved. It is a resting on
something without us, not a confidence concerning something within us.

3. Perhaps a still more common misunderstanding of faith
is to confound it with orthodoxy, with a vigorous zeal
for certain doctrines or formal statements of doctrine.

---

2. See Hebrews 6:19.

But Christian faith is fundamentally not belief of a creed, but belief in a person. It is not a zeal for a party, but confidence in the Lord. It embraces truth, but it is truth as enunciated and explained by him, "the truth as it is in Jesus."[3] It is not slavish submission to a routine of ceremonies, or a bigoted adherence to some doctrinal formulary, but a personal acceptance of Jesus Christ as Master and Teacher, as Savior and King. It includes the acceptance of the doctrines he taught as pure truth; for was not he the teacher who came from God? It includes the humble effort to live the life that he lived; for was not he our pattern, our example, our forerunner? It includes reliance on him for divine forgiveness and daily help and ultimate deliverance from sin; for he was exalted to be a Prince and a Savior, to give repentance and remission of sin. We believe testimony; we believe in our Lord. We believe Matthew and Mark and Luke and John; we believe in Jesus Christ. And by believing in him, not in ourselves, not in any creed or church or priest or ritual, we are saved.

It is evident, then, that by firm faith something more is meant than simply correct or settled belief, something more than unswerving adhesion to a form of doctrine. It is a living principle that overcomes the world, that lifts us above the world, that unites us to God, that gives us strength here and glory here after. It is personal resting on Jesus Christ. Hence it gives not a groundless, but a well-grounded assurance of union with him. In the words of an old hymn that I used to hear my father sing with great delight:

---

3. See Ephesians 4:21.

> And when I'm to die, 'Receive me' I'll cry;
> For Jesus hath loved me, I cannot tell why;
> But this I do find, we two are so joined,
> He'll not live in glory and leave me behind.[4]

Such a faith as this is not an inert, inactive, sleepy thing. It implies energy, responsibility. It involves trust both ways. Paul speaks, in that last letter of his to Timothy, of two deposits—that which we have committed to Jesus, and that which he has committed to us.[5] Both are sure, secured by the same mighty love and grace. Surely he will keep my deposit; surely the Captain may depend on me.

In one of the severest battles of the Civil War, a little squad of men stood among their slain on a commanding position, a mere fragment left. The storm of battle had just swept beyond them. A general officer came rushing up.

"Where is your colonel?"

"Dead."

"Where is your captain?"

"There he lies." (That captain was the son of my old and dear friend, A. M. Poindexter[6]).

"What are you doing here?"

---

4. John Gambold (d. 1771), "O tell me no more of this world's vain store," stanza 4. On Gambold, see Joseph Belcher, *Historical Sketches: Hymns, Their Writers, and Their Influence* (Philadelphia: Lindsay & Blakiston, 1859), 154–156. Some books ascribe this hymn to William Walker (1809–1875). Manly, however, included the hymn in his *The Baptist Psalmody* (1850) and ascribed it to Gambold (hymn 501).

5. See 2 Timothy 1:12 and 14.

6. See above, page 140 n. 4.

"He told us to hold this point to the last, and we are doing just what he said."

There is something grand in finishing the work and fulfilling the plans of those who have toiled and fallen by our side, and have gone up higher. We are conscious of renewed consecration and zeal whenever we think of such men as Judson and Wayland, of Fuller and Boyce[7]— of carrying out the work of such fathers as some of us have had.[8] But in our Christian enterprises we have a nobler encouragement. Blessed be God, we are not simply obeying the word of a dead and loved commander, who can no longer lead or help us; but of One who, though he died for us, lives again, and lives forever. We will hold this fort, for he is yonder, and signals to us still that he depends on us, and that we may depend on him.

---

7. Adoniram Judson (1788–1850), the American Baptist missionary to Burma; Francis Wayland (1796–1865), the Baptist president of prestigious Brown University; Richard Fuller (1804–1876), a well-known Baltimore Baptist minister who served as president of the Southern Baptist Convention on two occasions; and, of course, Manly's co-worker, James P. Boyce.

8. A reference to Basil Manly, Sr. This statement says much about the younger Manly's esteem of his father.

31

Contemporary worship reproved[1]

For some years it has been apparent that the rage for novelties in singing, especially in our Sunday-schools, has been driving out of use the old, precious, standard hymns. They are not memorized as of old. They are scarcely sung at all. They are not even contained in the undenominational song-books which in many churches have usurped the place of our old hymn books.

We cannot afford to lose these old hymns. They are full of the Gospel; they breathe the deepest emotions of pious hearts in the noblest strains of poetry; they have been tested and approved by successive generations of those that loved the Lord; they are the surviving fittest ones from thousands of inferior productions; they are hallowed by abundant usefulness and tenderest memories. But the young people of to-day are unfamiliar with them, and will seldom hear many of them, if the present tendency goes unchecked.

It has been the desire of many that a cheap and handy

---

1. Basil Manly, Jr., preface to *The Choice: A New Selection of Approved Hymns for Baptist Churches with Music* (Louisville: Baptist Book Concern, 1892), iii.

volume should be prepared containing the hymns which by common consent are approved and indispensable, and presenting a sufficient variety to meet ordinary necessities in public worship and in private devotion, as at baptism, the Lord's Supper, funerals, family worship, revivals, and the like.

Having compiled heretofore two hymn books, "The Baptist Psalmody," and "Baptist Chorals," and having had some share as an adviser in two others of our most popular books, my attention has been directed specially to the subject of hymnology all my ministerial life. I think I know what our people need, and what they desire. To meet that need and that desire the present work is offered. It is cheap, and of convenient size for the pocket; it contains no trash, and no unreal sentiment or unsound doctrine; and while of course in so small a collection many good hymns and some general favorites must be omitted, not one is inserted which is not judged worthy of a special place among the *choice* hymns of the language.

In arranging the music, I have endeavored to select the best of all the old, solid, standard tunes, which have been proved by experience, and often consecrated by tenderest associations. Many of them, though old and classic, will have all the attraction of novelty to the present generation. Some modern tunes which are familiar and excellent would gladly have been used; but they are held under the laws of copyright and could not be procured except at heavy expense, if at all. And this would have conflicted with the design of publishing a cheap book, within the reach of all. In a few cases, to meet an apparent necessity, the editor has inserted music of his own composition, for which he asks a lenient judgment.

Many churches have needlessly contented themselves with a very small number of tunes. With a very little effort, the whole congregation could be induced to learn every tune in this book, and have an ample variety for all occasions. Frequently a favorite tune is customarily wedded to several different hymns. There may be disappointment at finding it set here to only one of them, and some less familiar tune put with the others. It was thought best to do this, however, rather than to reprint the same tune several times. I wished to give as many really good tunes as the space would hold. No tune has been inserted which is not thought well worth learning.

Acknowledgements are due to several friends, especially to W. H. Doane of Cincinnati, Mus. Doct., who has contributed, I think more than any one of our time and country to ennoble and enrich our sacred music.[2] His advice and assistance have not only been cordially and gratuitously rendered, but have been most highly valued.

Two great ends have been kept steadily in view. One is to promote universal congregational singing: "Let all the

---

2. W. H. Doane (1832–1915) was president of J. A. Fay & Co., manufacturers of woodworking machinery, and was an extremely successful businessman and philanthropist. He also served as Sunday School superintendent and choir director at the Mount Auburn Baptist Church in Cincinnati, Ohio. Despite his busy life, he found time to compose over 2,000 hymn tunes during his lifetime. For a fuller discussion of Doane's life and contribution to church music in the nineteenth century, see J. H. Hall, *Biography of Gospel Song and Hymn Writers* (New York: Fleming H. Revell, 1914), 77–81.

people praise God." The other is to do something towards the elevation and general culture of musical and poetic taste among the Baptist people whom I love, and to whom the best labors of my life have been given. May God bless this effort, and build up our churches in pure doctrine, and fervent piety, for Jesus' sake. Amen.

Louisville, Kentucky
January, 1892